Playing the Long Game

Discover and Sustain Your Motivation as a School Leader

Scott A. Laliberte

Solution Tree | Press
a division of Solution Tree

555 North Morton Street
Bloomington, IN 47404
800.733.6786 (toll free) / 812.336.7700
FAX: 812.336.7790

email: info@SolutionTree.com
SolutionTree.com

Visit **go.SolutionTree.com/leadership** to download the free reproducibles in this book.

Printed in the United States of America

FSC
www.fsc.org
MIX
Paper | Supporting responsible forestry
FSC® C008955

Library of Congress Cataloging-in-Publication Data
Names: Laliberte, Scott A. author
Title: Playing the long game : discover and sustain your motivation as a school leader / Scott A. Laliberte.
Description: Bloomington, IN : Solution Tree Press, [2027] | Includes bibliographical references and index.
Identifiers: LCCN 2026005628 (print) | LCCN 2026005629 (ebook) | ISBN 9798893740936 paperback | ISBN 9798893740943 ebook
Subjects: LCSH: Educational leadership | School management and organization
Classification: LCC LB2806 .L22 2027 (print) | LCC LB2806 (ebook)
LC record available at https://lccn.loc.gov/2026005628
LC ebook record available at https://lccn.loc.gov/2026005629

Solution Tree
Cameron L. Rains, CEO
Edmund M. Ackerman, President

Solution Tree Press
Publisher: Kendra Slayton
Associate Publisher: Todd Brakke
Acquisitions Director: Hilary Goff
Editorial Director: Laurel Hecker
Art Director: Rian Anderson
Managing Editor: Sarah Ludwig
Copy Chief: Jessi Finn
Senior Production Editor: Sarah Foster
Copy Editor: Jessica Starr
Proofreader: Elijah Oates
Text and Cover Designer: Rian Anderson
Content Development Specialist: Amy Rubenstein
Associate Editor: Elijah Oates
Editorial Assistant: Madison Chartier

This book is dedicated with love and respect to my father, Paul Laliberte, and posthumously to my mother, Carol Laliberte. Few truly appreciate the sacrifices my parents have made and the love they have brought into the world by providing homes for adoptive children, such as your humble author.

ACKNOWLEDGMENTS

Long ago, my grandfather told me that I could learn something from everyone I meet in life and that it is important to watch and listen carefully to each person along the way. This advice has proven to be true. Therefore, recognizing all those who have contributed to this book and any experiences that brought it about would extend far beyond the space available. After all, through more than thirty-five years as an educator, my thinking has been impacted by thousands of teachers, professors, colleagues, students, and community members with whom I've had the privilege of interacting. I hope not to offend anyone through omission; though, I feel compelled to acknowledge a few of those people who formed my thoughts about the subject of this book.

I would like to extend my gratitude to four individuals whose voices featured prominently in my thinking as both a building and a systems leader in education. First, thanks to Paul MacMillan, who taught me never to shrink from a conflict in which I knew I was right. Thanks, as well, to Mark Joyce, who taught me to always blend situational awareness and diplomacy. Also, I thank Sandra McGonagle for her consistent example of the mutual importance of compassion and strength. Finally, sincere thanks to Nathan S. Greenberg for countless nature walks and lessons regarding the importance of strong principles to leaders of all kinds. Each of these educational leaders should count me among their most grateful pupils.

I am also grateful to so many of my colleagues in the community of school leaders here in New Hampshire who have supported my desire to bring balance and well-being to such difficult work. Specifically, thanks to Mark MacLean and Jerry Frew, with the New Hampshire School Administrators Association, for recognizing the value in these ideas. Thanks, as well, to Terry Donovan O'Dell—a teacher, mentor, and friend, who introduced me to the value of authentic reflection and retreat so many years ago. Thanks, once again, to good friend Brian Blake for long conversations on leadership and well-being, held in all manner of shady places and near bodies of water. Thanks to Jonathan Vander Els for his invaluable insights and continuing support in this interesting work. I also appreciate the ongoing support and encouragement of good friends, including Peter Curro, for the periodic reality checks; Adam Whitehouse Mullen, for reminding me of the value of boundless energy and hope; and Kent Hemingway, for exemplifying the value of foundational optimism blended with humility. Thanks, as well, to the crew of the Lake Pirates, for the much-needed laughs, reality checks, and periodic respite.

As always, I am grateful to those members of my family who have supported this project. I am so blessed to be surrounded by family who indulge my eccentricities. Each, in their own way, has supported and advanced the development of this book, from my daughter and stepdaughters to my siblings and in-laws. This is lonely work, and I have no idea how I might ever have typed out a word without their encouragement. Most of all, I wish to thank my amazing wife, Suzanne, who has always been a constant source of support and inspiration throughout this process. She is my strongest advocate, the love of my life, and the best friend I have ever had.

Finally, I am grateful that the editorial board at Solution Tree saw the value of this topic and that they were willing to support its development. I extend my deep gratitude to editors Laurel Hecker and Sarah Foster for their patience with me as we worked through drafts, as well as to the production team for lending their talents to develop this final product. Their professionalism and creativity have rendered a book that we can all be proud of.

Solution Tree Press would like to thank the following reviewers:

Janet Gilbert
Principal
Constitution Elementary School
Phoenix, Arizona

Erik D. Hermansen
Principal
Fivay High School
Hudson, Florida

Jed Kees
Director of School
Improvement Services
CESA 4
West Salem, Wisconsin

Laura Kollat
K–4 Director of
Student Development
Bio-Med Science Academy
Ravenna, Ohio

Elizabeth Love
Principal
Spradling Elementary School
Fort Smith, Arkansas

Luke Spielman
Principal
Park View Middle School
Mukwonago, Wisconsin

Nadine Trépanier-Bisson
Executive Director
Ontario Principals Council
Toronto, Ontario, Canada

Steven Weber
Assistant Principal
Rogers Heritage High School
Rogers, Arkansas

Bryn Williams
Principal
Coquitlam (School District No. 43)
Vancouver, British Columbia, Canada

Visit **go.SolutionTree.com/leadership** to download the free reproducibles in this book.

TABLE OF CONTENTS

Reproducibles are in italics.

ABOUT THE AUTHOR

Scott is a career educational leader, consultant, presenter, and leadership coach. He believes passionately in the impact school leaders have on both student learning and the long-term sustainability of educational systems. He has over thirty-five years of experience in schools, having spent time as a teacher, curriculum administrator, principal, and superintendent in New Hampshire. In 2022, he made a professional transition from working in schools to advancing the development of educational leaders. Scott currently works with both aspiring and practicing leaders through his consultancy, Standard Shift Consulting, LLC.

Throughout his career, Scott has demonstrated his strong belief in how school leadership impacts student learning, ranging from his long tenure as a member of the board of directors at the New Hampshire School Administrators Association to his frequent professional development presentations on leader well-being and skill development. He has presented across the United States on leadership capacity and has served as a mentor to many new leaders. Prior to writing for Solution Tree, Scott has written recreationally for many years, having published two short stories with the New Hampshire Writers' Project Anthology of Teachers' Writing, an article for the *New Hampshire Journal of Education*, a script for a children's summer theater production of a musical, and a self-published novel in 2006. Following his 2025 book, *The School Leader's Game Plan: Strategies for Maximizing Your Capacity to Tackle Daily Challenges*, with Solution Tree, this is his second book on the topic of school leadership.

Scott gained exposure to competitive athletics as a member of the University of New Hampshire football team, where he was a two-year starter on the offensive line and received all-conference honors following his senior season. He went on to share those experiences with student athletes as a high school football, basketball, and track coach. He strongly believes that cocurricular activities are fundamental to facilitating student growth and development.

Scott holds a bachelor of arts in English from the University of New Hampshire, a master's degree in education in school administration from Plymouth State University, and a certificate of advanced graduate study in educational leadership from Plymouth State University. He lives in the Lakes Region of New Hampshire with his wife, Suzanne.

To learn more about Scott's work, follow @scottlalib7122 on X, scottlalib on Facebook, Scott Laliberte on LinkedIn, and scottandrew7 on Instagram.

To book Scott A. Laliberte for professional development, contact pd@SolutionTree.com.

INTRODUCTION

Have you ever walked to your car at the end of a long day feeling exhausted and shrouded by the thought that you aren't sure you can keep doing this work? You wouldn't be a school or district leader if you hadn't. The work is challenging and relentless, the expectations are high, and the pressure to perform is considerable—both self-imposed and external. You learn that the work requires you to power through such moments, and they exact a toll over time. From thoughts to doubts, magnified by cognitive overload and exhaustion, it is a wonder that you indulge more serious questions about the state of your motivation.

For an element that holds such a pivotal piece of your ability to work each day, your motivation—and the factors behind it—dwells largely beneath conscious thought. After all, very few people begin each day by intentionally reflecting on the current state of their motivation. People tend to see it as something that simply ebbs and flows with time and something over which you have little control. This is not true, and that premise is a foundational belief in this book. You can exert influence over the source of and your level of motivation by giving it conscious attention. You can understand where your motivation comes from, how it takes form each day, and how best to maintain it over the course of your career. To do this requires intention, short-term discomfort, and a structured commitment to tangible outcomes. This book is committed to guiding you on a path to this outcome over the many hills and valleys of your career as a school leader. This is crucial work, and you are needed in the profession to guide your students and staff.

My first book, *The School Leader's Game Plan* (Laliberte, 2025), looked at the concept of leadership capacity by drawing parallels between the professional development of educational leaders and the training of competitive athletes. It began by acknowledging that leading schools is incredibly difficult and unlikely to become less so in the coming years. The task for leaders is to change how they prepare and sustain themselves through the challenges. By broadening the scope of leaders' professional development efforts, they become more resilient, healthy, and capable of overcoming challenges inherent in their work as school leaders.

While I sincerely hope that my previous book has helped many in education approach their capacity differently, researching and writing it left me with one troubling realization: Much of the material designed to support school leaders' motivation isn't sufficient or doesn't consider the practical realities of leading in education. Therefore, this book's concept emerged quickly—a practical and implementable approach to remain motivated given the specific challenges that confront educational leaders every day.

The Power of Story

Stories are used to structure memories, convey values, teach lessons, and remember what's most important (Storr, 2020). People use stories to remember things, to represent larger values and ideas, and to anticipate future events in a more efficient manner. In *The Science of Storytelling*, author Will Storr (2020) points out that the brain is a story processor and not a logic processor, concluding that:

> Turning the confusing and random into a comprehensible story is the essential function of the storytelling brain. We're surrounded by a tumult of often chaotic information. In order to help us feel in control, brains radically simplify the world with narrative. (Storr, 2020, p. 49)

In other words, humans construct a series of stories to create order in the chaos.

Another consideration is that people's brains are ideally suited for storytelling. For example:

> The human brain is wired to detect patterns. When we encounter information, the pattern-making hippocampus works to arrange it into logical sequences and narratives. In this way, stories serve as contextual organizers that help turn disjointed information into meaningful episodes. (Westover, 2024)

In this context, your own stories can help you understand how your brain stores pertinent information over the arc of your life. For example, if you want to understand what is most important to you, start with the stories that define you. If you want to gain insight into your values to understand what motivates you, turn to the stories you've stored away.

Where do you begin examining your own stories? Start with the story of your journey in school leadership. Think of the most challenging day you've had as a school leader. If it's not an entire day, then consider the most challenging moment you've had. If you're either new to the profession or contemplating a move into it, picture the largest challenge you've ever seen another leader go through. The complex school environment is rife with opportunities for challenge and conflict. It's not difficult to conjure up a series of incidents, moments, or days that have extended you beyond what you thought you could handle.

Now, think about the morning following that situation. You got back up, got ready for work, and you showed up again. You may not have wanted to go. You may have even contemplated walking away from the role altogether, but you went. Think, just for a moment, about why you went. What made you overcome any impulse you felt to stay home? In this book, I offer stories from the competitive sports world to help you draw insights into staying motivated amid the challenges of leading schools and districts. Start with this classic story about Jesse Owens.

The Story of a Motivated Athlete: Jesse Owens

Competitive sports offer a poignant opportunity to examine the foundational elements of motivation, from what it is based on to how it is expressed. While there are thousands of excellent examples of highly motivated athletes overcoming considerable challenges, few are as inspiring as the story of Jesse Owens, a Black, American track and field athlete in the 1930s (Jesse Owens Trust, n.d.).

Owens represented the United States in the 1936 Olympic Games in Berlin, Germany, which Adolph Hitler framed as a showcase for his ideas on white supremacy. Though surrounded by voices at home and abroad demeaning his worth as a human being and as an athlete, Owens was able to reach deep inside himself and find the strength to shine as a world champion in his sport. He won four gold medals, and it would be another fifty years before another athlete duplicated this feat (Jesse Owens Trust, n.d.).

Owens' story exemplifies the values of perseverance and the desire to sustain human dignity in the face of unimaginable adversity. The courage and strength he embodied on the track still serve as an example to millions of people. Just as his story carries forward a context for these ideals, so do the stories that shape your values, priorities, and view of the world. As you move ahead in both finding and preserving

> the source of your motivation to lead schools, the doorways to those insights can be found in your stories. Certainly, the story of Jesse Owens sets a high bar, yet he provides a perfect starting point at the intersection of sports and school leadership.
>
> While school leadership challenges are vastly different in scope, you can look at Owens as an example of someone driven by the strength of his ideals through great challenges. School leadership will test your strength and resilience, and your ability to withstand these tests depends on a strong awareness of what is most important to you. Owens confronts unimaginable resistance and challenges in his pursuit of athletic achievement, but he perseveres with both athletic success and as an example of strength and courage. The ideals that he embodies sustain him through the social injustices and discrimination he encounters each day. School leaders can learn much from this orientation to higher principles to propel them through daily challenges.

Assuming a position of school leadership is not compulsory. You choose to take on the responsibilities of the role, and you continue to show up each day. The reasons why you make this choice form the foundation of your motivation. Here lies an important distinction between the source of your motivation and your volition. What motivates you to act is generally the reason you make a choice in each moment. Your volition is the value, or the root cause, of that choice. For example, you may choose to take on a challenging job because it offers more money—that's your motivation. Upon further consideration, you may find that the source of your volition is the sense of responsibility you feel to provide for your family.

The Power of Your Story

At the heart of this book, there is a simple belief that the demands of leading schools often deny leaders the opportunity and format to engage in authentic reflection. This lack of reflection disconnects leaders from their volition and motivation, making burnout and attrition far more likely. While authentic reflection occurs in various ways for different people, it helps you clearly see your reasons for engaging in the challenges of this work and sustains your fire in the face of it.

This book offers a structured approach, intended to support and sustain your motivation, that you can adapt to your reflective practices. It examines the long-term benefits of active awareness of the sources of your motivation and volition.

They aren't always the same, but they are usually related. Stay connected to what motivates you, and the volition behind that choice, and you'll drastically increase both your effectiveness in your role and the likelihood that you will continue within it.

However, when you can't stay connected to your motivation—especially when you need to make difficult decisions, you find yourself in a hopeless situation, or you run headlong into a frustrating obstacle—you may find yourself trudging on out of duty, or you may walk away. In other words, when you no longer find yourself driven by a purpose that you value, you will make decisions other than to lead. Whether by going through the motions in their current position or walking away altogether, school leaders who find themselves disconnected from their sense of purpose will struggle with motivation. This work is too challenging to do without a clear sense of purpose. Your work as an educational leader requires a close awareness of the ideals that guide your decisions.

To begin this journey and support your storytelling mind, you'll focus on understanding your motivation and volition using what this book calls your seven stories. Each story you write contains elements of your journey as an educator and your decision to lead within the profession. These stories are common to most of us, though the details are personal.

Recalling stories that shape your experiences as a school leader can clarify your values. Therefore, at each chapter's start, you'll find a prompt for one of the seven stories that relate to some pivotal element of your journey. Within each of these stories, you'll identify concepts, experiences, and values that you have developed over your time as an educator. Each chapter also contains reflection questions that are intended to guide a deeper recollection of your experiences. The intent is for you to recall details and use them to understand your values more completely.

No matter how long you've been working in the profession, you will have some form of experience relative to these story prompts, and your resulting stories inform a deeper understanding of why you made each choice along the way. These stories contain the foundational values that have guided you both to become an educator and to lead within schools or districts. As outlined earlier, the brain stores these crucial concepts in story form, both to link to related concepts and to recall as required. The pace of your work as a leader restricts your access to these ideas, but intentional exercises can unearth these concepts.

The aim in writing your seven stories is to slow down your thought process and facilitate a more authentic connection to your fundamental motivations to lead.

By building a more comprehensive understanding of your motivation, you can more proactively sustain it as you move through the challenging work of leading schools and educational systems. To help with that, you will build a structured approach to reflect on the underlying patterns that form your volition. Like with many instructional approaches, there are clear procedures for writing the seven stories that include the flexibility to personalize and differentiate the learning.

Each of the following seven story prompts focuses on a key element of your career as a school leader. These stories progress chronologically, from your initial entry into the education profession to your emergence as a leader. They give context to key components of your work—specifically to those moments that reveal parts of your volition as an educational leader. In each story, core elements will guide you along the way, helping you recall key factors that substantiate why you do what you do.

1. **Entering Your Rookie Year:** Where do you come from? This story helps you describe your origin.
2. **Playing for Keeps:** When did you choose to pursue education as a career? This story identifies core values that brought you to this profession.
3. **Coaching From the Sidelines:** What caused you to accept your first leadership position? This story identifies your call to action as a leader.
4. **Reassessing Your Playbook:** What are the three most important achievements of your overall career thus far? This story describes core values and how they change over the arc of your life.
5. **Leaning Into Your Team:** Can you identify a time when you were extremely upset by a situation that violated your ethics or professional boundaries on the job? This story identifies your passions and principles and helps you understand where your ethical lines are.
6. **Changing Teams:** What would cause you to walk away from your profession? This story identifies areas relative to sustaining yourself within the profession.
7. **Hanging the Championship Banner:** What are the most fulfilling rewards of your work? This story identifies the outcomes that you value most and the priorities behind them.

While these stories don't comprise an exhaustive list, you likely will find other stories during reflection that further clarify the source of your motivation.

How the Book Is Structured

This book intends to bring concrete and actionable form to the abstract concept of personal motivation, which is why it centers on the seven stories. Although you'll find reflective prompts and activities throughout the book, this does not mean that all materials are for everyone because this is a personal journey. Engage in those experiences that are most meaningful for you.

Chapter 1 investigates the nature of motivation from a psychological standpoint. This chapter focuses on the larger psychological concepts surrounding motivation rather than diving into specific theories and models. Begin with the first of the seven stories, "Entering the Rookie Year," which prompts you to establish context for your choice of education as a profession. Prior to understanding your motivation to lead, begin with an awareness of previous life experiences that brought you to this profession. Chapter 1 aims to build a framework to sustain your motivation.

Chapter 2 examines the biology of motivation. Thanks to advances in neurobiology, brain imaging, and a deeper understanding of the chemistry of life, there is now more practical knowledge of how the human body is inspired to move. This overview allows you to see how physiological variables impact your sense of motivation and volition. The choices you make and the actions you take are guided by brain chemistry; forming a fundamental understanding of it allows you to see this impact each day. In "Playing for Keeps," the story prompt asks you to recall the actual circumstances and values that led you to choose your first position as an educator. Here, a working knowledge of the biology of motivation becomes crucial as you project your career path in a sustainable direction. By understanding how your brain makes decisions, you gain crucial insights into both your thought process and the outcomes. Awareness of these influences allows you to manage them during more challenging moments.

Chapter 3 asks you to begin building your individual model for understanding and sustaining those factors that motivate you. The "Coaching From the Sidelines" prompt aims to focus your reflection specifically on your choice to lead. This reflection distinguishes your work as an educator from the more specific motivational elements associated with leading. All of your colleagues chose to become educators, but far fewer stepped into leadership roles. This reflection starts to build a personalized support network for your motivation. By examining the roots of your choices, you will discover fundamental values that guide these choices and form your behavior patterns. Over the course of your career, this support network will help with your longevity as a school leader.

Chapter 4 confronts the reality of how your motivation changes with your experience and growth. The story prompt "Reassessing Your Playbook" will help you identify your three most important achievements of your overall career, which will help you understand your core values and how they change over the arc of your life. Values form the foundational elements of motivation and volition, and values also evolve as life circumstances change. A thoughtful approach to maintaining motivation recognizes these changes and helps you understand what drives you to evolve. Making ongoing self-understanding a part of your practice is the best way to monitor these different chapters of your life. Whether as an annual process or as a response to significant life events, there is always a benefit to recognizing transitions in what you value and how you make decisions.

Chapter 5 examines the different expectations of school leadership and acknowledges the impact of long-term stress and energy depletion across the scope of your career. In the story prompt "Leaning Into Your Team," you will describe a time when you were extremely upset by a situation that violated your ethics or professional boundaries on the job. These situations, and the principles behind them, indicate your outer limits and issues of personal passion that wear on you over time. Being aware of these boundaries can help you avoid attrition. You will look at the ever-changing lines that separate work challenge from burnout and the difficult decisions that accompany both moments. Here again, the environments in which you lead also evolve over time; priorities and demands change due to social dynamics and political environments. Being aware of your energy depletion and how close you are to burnout can let you know when to turn to external sources of support to stay motivated. There are many customs and professional resources available to you within the community of school leaders, and don't be afraid to lean on your friends during moments of need. When you are feeling empty within, it is time to look for support without.

Chapter 6 examines the nature of change and the progression of school leaders from role to role over the course of their careers. Progressing to different leadership roles ensures that experienced leaders occupy positions that are best suited for them and that leaders remain engaged and fulfilled. Leaders, like schools, change over time, and they are expected to either grow within a role or advance to another that is more compatible with who they are. In the story prompt "Changing Teams," you will consider what would cause you to walk away from your role. This story prompt differentiates between those matters that require perseverance and those that necessitate a change of role or location. Recognizing when it is time to dig in and fight or when it's time to make a change are both foundational elements of leadership.

Chapter 7 is a deep dive into developing a personalized approach to authentic reflection and maintaining motivation as school leaders carry the burdens expected of them each day. The process comes full circle in the last story, explicitly stating those elements of your work that move you. In the story prompt "Hanging the Championship Banner," you'll describe the most fulfilling rewards of your work. You will also take a deeper look into the concept of retreats, both as a personal matter and as part of broader school leadership, and strategies for planning retreat experiences that are authentic and productive. The chapter intends for you to conclude the book with a personalized approach best suited to your needs and the expectations of the environment in which you lead.

In the middle of your darkest and most challenging moments, be consciously aware of why you do what you do. Your continued impact on the lives of your students depends on it.

CHAPTER 1

Finding Your Motivation

> **Entering the Rookie Year**
>
> Where do you come from? (This story helps you describe your origin.) Life experiences are at the root of most things that motivate leaders. The experiences you recall first or most frequently likely impact you more and may provide greater value in understanding why you choose to do what you do.

Anyone with a background in athletics or an interest in sports stories—for example, the popular TV show *Ted Lasso* or classic films such as *Hoosiers* or *Remember the Titans*—can recall the archetypal coach delivering a pregame speech that thrills even a passive listener. The coach's passion when giving the speech, vocal cadence and emphasis, emphatic body language, and the universal message move people. One example is when, in a speech before an important game, coach Ted Lasso extols the value of belief in oneself to his team, saying, "Belief doesn't just happen 'cause you hang something on the wall. It comes from here [heart], you know? Up here [brain] and down here [gut]" (Lee & Lipsey, 2023). Here, the coach appeals to the members of his team to rally their morale and build their confidence before the big match.

The following are some common themes in these pregame speeches.

- Shared values, such as the importance of self-sacrifice for the team's collective success
- Confidence rooted in moments of individual growth or collective efficacy of the team
- Eventual rewards inherent in successful competition, either in victory or in personal or collective growth
- Value of hard work, dedication to details, or overcoming adversity

In these game-oriented speeches, the coach does not necessarily instill that value in team members but instead contextualizes values that individual team members already have within a particular moment of competition. One example involves Ted Lasso instructing one of his players to "be a goldfish" because he says that goldfish have a ten-second memory and to forget mistakes or miscues in a game in the interest of being resilient (Kelly & Braff, 2020).

The pregame speech's inspirational appeal is present in school leadership as well. You are surrounded by stories and individuals who embody values that are important to you, and the way you encounter these narratives forms an important element of your motivation. For example, the collective value for aiding individual student learning may motivate you to provide unique accommodations or supports to a student in crisis. While the delivery and composition of these moments may not necessarily have the same dramatic impact as that of an animated speech, the concept is the same. You can find strength and motivation in the embodiment of shared values. By identifying these values in action, you propel yourself and others to act in a manner consistent with them. As you try to understand the power of shared values, this chapter provides a working definition of motivation as a concept, the roots of your motivation to be an educational leader, and the psychology of motivation.

As you look at the details of your origin story, you will find examples of traits that form your values. For example, your life may have been impacted positively by an educator from your own days as a student, and as you looked at potential professions, you recalled the feelings of affirmation or purpose that accompanied that relationship. Perhaps, as you sought out your purpose, you saw a career path featuring that potential. Therefore, you were motivated to explore education as a profession because of the positive impact you encountered as a student.

Pause for Reflection

To establish some of the important and formative elements for who you are as a person, describe two or three significant life experiences that drew you to education as a profession. Focus on your life experiences before work—such as your childhood, educational experiences, life events, and so on—that may have been important to forming you as a person.

The Meaning of Motivation

For a topic that seems to be self-evident to leaders, the process of defining motivation becomes complex very quickly. So, what is motivation? One definition is, "the condition of being eager to act or work" (Motivation, n.d.). Your motivation exists in whatever causes you to act. It's what gets you moving. From that simple phrase comes the two factors that introduce the complexities both in understanding motivation and staying motivated over time. First, what causes you to move forward? In other words, where does your motivation come from? Another consideration is that one person's source of motivation can be so different from another's. People also evolve over their lifetimes, so time could be a factor here. What motivates you during one time in your life may not during another. How can this source of motivation change over time, or can it remain constant?

Second, what does that source of motivation get you moving toward? For example, in your origin story, your previous experience or mindset likely caused you to act. Therefore, what you are motivated to do is as personal to you as the cause of that motivation. This book looks specifically at school leaders and their motivation both to accept a position of leadership in schools and to carry out those responsibilities over time. In the broader sense, the decision to assume and retain a position of school leadership can be considered as a single component, yet there are many different roles and circumstances within school leadership that impact the motivation equation. You can choose to move into other positions of leadership. You can choose to lead in a similar role in another place. You can also choose to step outside of leadership altogether. Your objective can also vary. Each leader chooses to enter the role, to enter a specific assignment, and at some point, to leave it driven by different factors or priorities.

Another distinction is the difference between *motivation* and *volition.* Although they are often used in similar contexts, there is a key distinction between them in this book. *Volition* refers to the act of choosing or the power to choose (Volition, n.d.). Where motivation identifies what causes you to take steps toward an outcome, volition goes a step deeper to look at the root causes behind what motivates you to make that choice. For example, you may be motivated to start an exercise program out of a desire to improve your overall health, but your volition may be rooted in your core value for fitness or maintaining an active lifestyle. In an example based in school leadership, a person may choose to become an administrator because they want to make a higher salary, and that decision may be rooted in the value of providing for their family. This subtle distinction becomes more important as you reflect on the factors that influence your personal motivation.

Because the factors that motivate you and the roles to which you aspire are so widely different, there is no specific guidance to help you become and remain motivated. Instead, in this situation, identify the factors that are important to you and use them to reflect on your own clear goals as a means of staying motivated over time. One example to illustrate this distinction is the matter of financial rewards. You may be motivated to work as a school principal for the higher salary, but the source of that motivation could be your desire to provide for your family. The financial reward gets you moving, but the volitional basis for the decision rests in your value of family. This process goes beyond the impact of a single activity or reflection and instead aspires to set forth practices that will keep you grounded in an authentic sense of purpose. The alternative is truly sad. There are few moments lonelier than when leaders ask themselves, "Why do I do this?" only to find themselves without an answer.

Therefore, as you move forward in this process, please know that the working definition of *motivation* that will guide you is, the factors that compel you to act toward a specific goal or outcome. Behind these factors live the roots of that choice—the values that form your volition. These elements will form the structure of this experience, such as the choices you make, the factors that compel you, and the goals to which you aspire.

Pause for Reflection

Many educators identify a person or people from their past who were instrumental in their own education and development. These people become important role models in forming your values. Name a mentor, teacher, or other person that you encountered as a young person that you consider a mentor or role model.

The Choice to Lead

At some point in your professional journey, you became intrigued with the idea of leading. You explored different roles, opportunities, and means of getting there. And then came a signpost moment. You chose to make the leap. You chose to assume a role of responsibility within the school community, most likely because of the same factors you identified in your origin story projected over a position of broader influence. Now, instead of caring for the students in your class, you impact all students in your school. In the most fundamental sense, leadership is a choice. More specifically, it is a series of choices that brought you either to a leadership role or to aspire to such a role. There are well-founded reasons that you chose this path and that you continue to walk it each day. These reasons are the very heart of your motivation.

The factors that can complicate your decision to assume a position of leadership, and to remain within it, dwell within the innate challenges of your work. Managing the wide variety of responsibilities and expectations of school or district leadership is no small task, as school leaders' days are filled with logistic challenges, moral dilemmas, interpersonal relationship management, and legal and policy compliance. Each day, school leaders confront the decision to continue working in this environment. It is no small wonder that turnover rates continue to challenge consistency in schools (Institute of Education Sciences, 2023).

A report by the National Center for Education Statistics (2024) differentiates attrition rates by stayers (retained), movers (change locations but stay in the same role), and leavers (exited the profession). This study differentiated between public and private school principals and found that, "Among those serving as principals during the 2020–21 school year, 11 percent of public school principals and 10 percent of private school principals had left the profession by the 2021–22 school year" (National Center for Educational Statistics, 2024). These turnover rates happen for different reasons. For some principals, the work may take place in poor working conditions. For others, they may have experienced insufficient preparation or professional development for the role. Still others may be cut out to be a principal but are not compensated fairly (Levin & Bradley, 2019). Ultimately, a leader must be motivated to enter the profession, to enter a role, and to remain there so long as they can sustain their effectiveness.

Educational leadership is not an easy path, but good people need to choose it so schools can prepare students for the complexities of this world. As you examine what is needed to develop and maintain motivation, you'll find that this book's approach builds around the fundamental reality that leadership is an ongoing series of choices.

The Psychology of Motivation

Now that you understand that leadership is founded on a series of choices, it's important to investigate the roots of motivation. This underscores the fundamental idea that both the sources of motivation and its outcomes are most certainly relative. You can frame your understanding of what motivates you in psychological terms, but the substance of that frame lies within your own mind. To understand your own motivation means embracing the personal reflective journey. While the term *reflection* is admittedly so overused within educational circles that it dilutes both the impact and meaning, stepping away from the demands of daily work to reflect on your broader status and scope is integral to sustaining your motivation. If you want to know what motivates you, you need the time and space to think deeply about the stories that have shaped you. Yes, understanding some of the different theories and concepts can guide you, but ultimately understanding your motivation will come from your ability to see different theories and apply them to your life.

Where do you start in building your understanding of what motivates you? Psychology divides motivation into two main categories: (1) intrinsic and (2) extrinsic (Dr. Ermshar & Associates, 2023). While these terms are likely familiar, providing clear definitions can build context.

Intrinsic motivation refers to any source of behavior that comes from within you—from your interests to your values or beliefs (Bandhu et al., 2024). Whenever you make a specific decision based on some element of your personality or as an outcome of your thoughts, you are intrinsically motivated. For example, if a school principal decides to remain in their position out of personal loyalty, or out of a commitment they've made to the school community, they are intrinsically motivated to that outcome. Their value for loyalty or commitment is what compels them to stay.

Extrinsic motivation comes from outside variables that influence your decisions (Bandhu et al., 2024). When your choices are guided by expected financial or material rewards, accolades, or affirmation, or to avoid some form of punishment or negative repercussion, you are extrinsically motivated. To continue from the previous example, if the principal remains in their position out of financial need, community affirmation, or a fear of what may happen if they leave, they are extrinsically motivated. Their choice to stay is based on a value for rewards that exist outside of themself.

Naturally, most school leaders are motivated by some combination of intrinsic and extrinsic factors—life and work are too complicated for neat categories—yet maintaining awareness of what personally motivates you forms a foundation for maintaining long-term motivation. At the end of this chapter, a reproducible worksheet, "Prioritizing Intrinsic Versus Extrinsic Motivation" (page 22), invites you to examine your own experiences and values from an intrinsic versus extrinsic perspective. This exercise provides a concrete opportunity for you to gain clearer awareness of what factors motivate you. This information can guide further reflection and planning as you move into the process of developing personalized plans to maintain your motivation.

After exploring intrinsic versus extrinsic motivation, consider different psychological perspectives of motivation. Some motivational psychologists theorize that motivation is grounded in need fulfillment, while others postulate that people are driven by subconscious constructs built by experiences over a lifetime. Therefore, according to these theories, your motivation is rooted in some form of subconscious influence, existing beneath your awareness, that sways your choices.

Another theory is *self-determination theory*, which is "a macro theory of human motivation that evolved from research on intrinsic and extrinsic motivations and expanded to include research on work organizations and other domains of life" (Deci, Olafsen, & Ryan, 2017). This theory transcends the simple, behaviorist ideas that explain motivation as a simple matter of rewards. In fact, it has "toppled the dominant belief that the best way to get human beings to perform tasks is to reinforce their behavior with rewards" (O'Hara, 2017). Therefore, this theory compels people to look inward to find factors that influence behavior.

Self-determination theory looks at the distinction between *autonomous motivation* (internalized) and *controlled motivation* (externalized) as well as three basic needs held by all employees: (1) competence, (2) autonomy, and (3) relatedness (Deci et al., 2017). This theory goes well beyond simply locating the intrinsic and extrinsic sources of motivation and integrates addressing common needs.

Researchers Edward L. Deci, Anja H. Olafsen, and Richard M. Ryan (2017) define *autonomous motivation* as being "characterized by people being engaged in an activity with a full sense of willingness, volition, and choice" (p. 20). In other words, people choose to engage in an activity that is of value to them. Deci and colleagues (2017) continue:

> When individuals understand the worth and purpose of their jobs, feel ownership and autonomy in carrying them out, and receive clear feedback and supports, they are likely to become more autonomously motivated and reliably perform better, learn better, and be better adjusted. (p. 20)

By contrast, *controlled motivation* is characterized as being externally located either through "... contingent rewards or power dynamics, the extrinsic focus that results can narrow the range of employees' efforts, produce short-term gains on targeted outcomes, and have negative spillover effects on subsequent performance and work engagement" (Deci et al., 2017, p. 20). While there can be intrinsic or extrinsic factors present in each of these types of motivation, the key distinction between them rests in where the impetus comes from. Are you acting on something that is important to you, or are you reacting to some external factor of lesser value?

Perhaps the best-known element of self-determination theory is that three core needs drive intrinsic motivation (Deci et al., 2017):

> Perhaps more importantly, [self-determination theory] propositions also focus on how social and cultural factors facilitate or undermine people's sense of volition and initiative, in addition to their well-being and the quality of their performance. Conditions supporting the individual's experience of autonomy, competence, and relatedness are argued to foster the most volitional and high-quality forms of motivation and engagement for activities, including enhanced performance, persistence, and creativity.

In this context, *autonomy* refers to your ability to make choices within your work environment. *Competence* indicates the importance of possessing the requisite skills and knowledge necessary to complete your work effectively. Finally, *relatedness* acknowledges the need for interpersonal connectedness and fellowship. Deci and Ryan maintain that these three ideas represent basic psychological needs shared by all people, and they form the basis of effective motivation across different environments (O'Hara, 2017).

These needs give context to some of the upcoming work in addressing volition in this book. To clarify this connection, the following applies the needs of self-determination theory to your work as a school leader.

- Autonomous or internalized motivation comes from your ability to determine your own path. You choose to lead, and you choose where and when to lead. Your ongoing awareness of this choice and the reasons behind it result in satisfaction with our need for autonomy.

For example, school leaders choosing to change either locations or roles within the profession are exercises of autonomy.

- The need for competence within the leadership role validates why you prioritize ongoing professional development focused on your greatest areas of need. For example, your ongoing desire for professional learning, beyond that which is required for credentialling, is an exercise of your need for competence.
- Relatedness highlights the basic need for connections with other people—both within the scope of your professional work and in your life beyond it. Leading in any environment can be a lonely proposition; you must fulfill your need for quality interpersonal relationships in a manner consistent with your personal values. For example, participation in professional networking opportunities, state or regional associations, or conferences represent a few opportunities available to school leaders to relate to peers and experience fellowship.

The deeply personal nature of motivation, and your own experiences and values that form it, certainly validates further exploration into motivational psychology. Advancing your knowledge in this complex area results in a deeper understanding of your own personal motivation.

Pause for Reflection

Often, your previous life challenges can be formative elements of your volition. Identify a challenge that you have been able to overcome on your road to becoming an educator. This could be a personal challenge, life circumstances, or any other hurdle that might have prevented you from graduating from college and entering the profession.

Conclusion

In this chapter, you have begun taking steps toward a more authentic and actionable understanding of the psychology of motivation and how it impacts your experiences each day. This information sets your limits and expectations of how you experience motivation and how you can best maintain it. It helps you understand why you think as you do and how you can best respond to your thoughts. Framing your reflections with the context of psychology sets the scene for the next chapter, which delves into the biochemistry of the brain.

To reiterate the good news, your career path is a choice, made within your own psychological constructs. No one is forced to become a leader of an educational institution. If you either occupy that role or are contemplating that direction, you are choosing it. Whether you succeed or fail, the degree of your effectiveness and the opportunities that await you are all completely different matters. It is the first step, the reason behind the choice, that sustains you.

Leaders can recognize factors that push them in any direction on their path in life. Maintaining a sense of self-awareness lets you recognize what motivates you. The forces behind your behavior that form your volition still result in you making a choice, which is an exercise of free will. With that choice comes a host of different factors; leaders do what they do for a lot of different reasons. Specifically, consider the choice to pursue a position of leadership within a school or district. There are a host of different decisions to be made along that path, starting with the initial exploration and proceeding through the career path ahead. Leaders choose preparation programs, to apply for and accept jobs, ways to work within them, and ultimately, when to leave the profession. (Though, admittedly, some leaders leave not of their own volition. They are forced to leave because of different choices they make—more on that later in the book.) Each choice is guided by some source of volition. Leaders choose each step for a reason. It is this very concept that forms the substance of motivation.

Running beneath the cognitive surface of your mind are different factors that influence your decision-making process. Some are obvious—you lean on logic to try to determine the outcomes of a decision. "If I do [action], [consequence] will happen." You examine what you know of the available options and decide based on that knowledge. Naturally, the process is a bit more complex than that. You also have different factors running beneath the surface that cause you to lean one way or another. Your value system pulls you in each direction, as do your experiences with similar outcomes in the past or your hopes for the future.

In any case, you evaluate the decisions that confront you using available information and your best conjecture regarding potential outcomes. You make the best decision you can, given those circumstances. In the context of assuming and remaining in a leadership position, circumstances change rapidly and evolve within a complex dynamic presented by the work. Not only are you called on to make decisions as a school leader but also to *be* a school leader. Decisions are inherent in the role and *remaining* in the role—both within our current assignment and in the profession.

Telling Your Story

You will find elements of your life experiences at the root of most things that motivate you. Those experiences that you recall first or most frequently can have greater value to you in understanding why you choose to do what you do. In the following space, craft your story for "Entering Your Rookie Year" by describing your upbringing, influential experiences, and impactful life events that have shaped who you are.

Prioritizing Intrinsic Versus Extrinsic Motivation

The following reflective activity encourages you to think about the different decisions you make during a typical day and the location of the factors that motivate your choices. The list of factors in the following figure is not intended to be exhaustive or comprehensive. Your perceptions and your responses may differ at different times. The goal is for you to recognize the difference between intrinsic and extrinsic factors that motivate you in each situation.

Consider each of the following actions within the context of your own thinking. Use the Your Influences? column to record your personal perspective on that action and whether you find yourself drawn more to intrinsic or extrinsic factors. Once completed, you can look back on your responses to see if you notice a pattern. While you will almost certainly include both intrinsic and extrinsic factors, you may notice certain circumstances that give insight into your motivation.

Action	Intrinsic Factors	Your Influences?	Extrinsic Factors
Accepting a job that pays more	Provide for family, feeling valued, security		Greater financial freedom, purchasing power for things you want, status
Changing jobs in the same profession, different location	Fresh new start, different working environment		Affirmation or opportunity for recognition
Stopping to assist a stranger in need	Positive contribution to a person in need		Recognized for being a good person
Traveling to an unfamiliar country on vacation	Challenge, personal development, enrichment		Social media posts, affirmation from friends

page 1 of 2

Action	Intrinsic Factors	Your Influences?	Extrinsic Factors
Buying a new car	Safety and security, fewer mechanical problems		Status or value perception
Giving a gift to a family member	Positive feelings for helping a loved one		Incur the favor or positive perception of someone close to you
Beginning a new exercise program	Personal challenge, healthy lifestyle		Look better, socialize
Upgrading your phone to the newest model	Value for features and reliability		Being perceived as technologically current
Taking a long hike in the countryside	Need for quiet and tranquility		Enjoying the company of fellow hikers
Buying new clothing for an upcoming important meeting	Internal feelings of confidence		Perception of professionalism by others
Visiting your parents	Maintaining an important family relationship		Need for their approval
Speaking out on a social issue of importance to you	Self-affirming action on an important matter		Perception by others of the strength of your conviction

CHAPTER 2

Exploring Motivation and Your Brain

> **Playing for Keeps**
>
> When did you choose to pursue education as a career? (This story identifies core values that brought you to this profession.) Most educators can recall the time, place, and circumstances in which they first decided to become an educator. For example, some aspired to become teachers when they were children, influenced by a mentor or meaningful adult relationship, while others came to the profession in early adulthood, inspired by the opportunity to affect change in students' lives.

A basic understanding of the human body is fundamental to training for a sport. For example, athletes learn early on which muscle groups are impacted by specific exercises or elements of training. They learn that the upper trapezius muscles that connect the head to the shoulders serve to protect the neck and allow it to move. It isn't necessary to have studied advanced anatomy or kinesiology to be an athlete, but it is helpful to have a basic understanding, including a command of common terms. Athletes can have targeted conversations about the composition and function of their bodies by understanding these terms. They learn to apply this working knowledge to training for their sport and the techniques associated with success within the sport.

So, what is the parallel to identifying the intricacies of motivation? Just as basic science guides athletes, a fundamental understanding of the brain's chemicals can help you see the biochemistry of what drives you. You need not be a biochemist or a physician; a conversational awareness of this part of brain functioning gives context for understanding the bigger picture. Just as quadricep muscles provide power to drive the body forward, your brain's chemical cocktail can spur you to action in a variety of circumstances. In this chapter, you will gain a fundamental awareness of how brain chemistry impacts your daily life in the fast-paced and stressful world of educational leadership.

Examining the starting point of your career can help you develop a clearer understanding of the roots of your motivation and volition. In the same way, a clearer understanding of those brain functions will allow you to understand *when* you are moved to act. A clear understanding of the origin of an act reveals much about the factors behind it.

Pause for Reflection

In the story prompt, "Playing for Keeps," you move from significant life events into your choice to pursue education as a career. Identify any significant choices along your path to becoming an educator, including your choice of academic major and your first job. Why did you begin your studies that led to teaching? What events led to you getting your first job?

The Role of Dopamine and Rewards in Your Choices

People don't *have* to go to the gym to exercise, but they choose to get off the couch and do so. Motivation is a conscious choice, which is different from the brain's unconscious processes that keep the heart beating. At the center of the choice to move lies a neurotransmitter called *dopamine*, which is "a neurotransmitter made in your brain. It plays a role as a 'reward center' and in many body functions, including memory, movement, motivation, mood, attention and more" (Cleveland Clinic, 2022a). A neurotransmitter performs its function in the brain when it "acts as a chemical messenger, communicating messages between nerve cells in your brain and the rest of your body" (Cleveland Clinic, 2022a). In other words, dopamine is the chemical that passes on important information within the brain and to the rest of the body.

While many people commonly associate dopamine as the source of pleasurable outcomes, it is more complicated than that. In *Dopamine Nation*, author Anna Lembke (2021) clarifies the role of this neurotransmitter:

> Dopamine is not the only neurotransmitter involved in reward processing, but most neuroscientists agree it is among the most important. Dopamine may play a bigger role in the motivation to get a reward than the pleasure of the reward itself. (p. 48)

In other words, dopamine moves you toward something. You receive the reinforcing effects of this chemical through your efforts more so than from the outcome.

Lembke (2021) continues to elaborate on the motivational elements of dopamine and the ways that various sources of it can form the foundational elements of addiction: "Dopamine is used to measure the addictive potential of any behavior or drug. The more dopamine a drug releases in the brain's reward pathway . . . and the faster it releases dopamine, the more addictive the drug" (p. 49). She explains that the pleasure produced by this process is balanced by an offsetting pain response as a way for the brain to maintain homeostatic balance. In fact, she explains that "neuroscientists have determined that pleasure and pain are processed in overlapping brain regions and work via an opponent-process mechanism" (Lembke, 2021, pp. 50–51). In the literal sense, people cannot experience pleasure without a resulting element of pain, which brings the brain back into balance.

This process explains the foundational element of addictive behavior; the more dopamine the brain produces, the bigger the crash afterward. The brain will seek more of whatever brought on the pleasure to escape the pain—thus, a cycle emerges (Lembke, 2021). While the topic of addiction is beyond the scope of this book, the way people are driven to act by the reward pathways in the brain is central to this discussion. The dopamine produced by the brain moves you to act with a promise of some form of reward at the outcome.

While a comprehensive understanding of the neurobiology of decision making requires a deep dive into the nervous system's physiology and chemistry, the goal here is only to understand the foundation of behavior. In that context, direct connection exists between dopamine and our formation of memories: "Dopamine also enhances reward-related memories. It strengthens synapses—the junctions where neurons pass messages—in the brain's learning and memory center, the hippocampus" (Halber, 2018). In other words, your brain stores memories that relate to previous rewarding experiences. You associate those memories with the corresponding rewards that accompanied them, and they serve you as you look ahead for similar experiences.

The following list identifies a series of healthy dopamine-producing activities you will find in your daily life. To identify more dopamine-producing activities, see the reproducible "A Dopamine Scavenger Hunt" on page 35.

- Exercise or do other physical movement (choose from your favorite activities; Huberman, 2022; Julson, 2025; Spiller, 2024).
- Have a solid night's sleep (Huberman, 2022).
- Complete a project that has been nagging you or compile a to-do list and start checking off tasks (Falkowski, 2016; Spiller, 2024).
- Choose interpersonal connections instead of computer-based ones (Spiller, 2024).
- Spend time in (or find) a community of people where you can feel a sense of belonging, such as common interests or activities (Spiller, 2024).

This list illustrates the variety of influences that dopamine has in your daily activities, as well as ideas for positive ways to add these experiences to your life. You can choose how you pursue rewarding experiences, and acknowledging the opportunity to pursue positive outcomes is a solid first step toward sustainable sources of motivation.

Just as with the broader scope of your life, you can find elements of your work that also produce dopamine and influence motivation. For example, the idea of pursuing interpersonal interactions rather than computer-based ones can also extend to your relationships within schools (Spiller, 2024). School leaders often rely on email as an expedient way to communicate with staff members or parents. While this gets the message out quickly, it does little to deepen your interpersonal relationships and your own need for connections. In-person communication can be worth the added time for deepening those relationships and meeting your own needs.

In a similar way, the notion of task completion as a positive dopamine producer (Falkowski, 2016; Spiller, 2024) can also be translated readily to your role as a school leader. By approaching your busy day with a clear and organized list of tasks, you can lighten your overall to-do list and create a dopamine response to carry you forward. Whether you have a list of managerial tasks, such as building oversight or budgeting, or a broader instructional leadership challenge, such as classroom observations, you can greatly benefit from a clear schedule of tasks and times for completion.

Let's discuss what rewards hold value for you as a school leader, which is one of the key factors supporting the need for authentic reflection and awareness of your seven stories. The work you do brings some form of fulfillment (reward). For example, school leaders find fulfillment in parts of the work including students attaining learning targets, a meaningful professional learning experience for staff, or a substantive community event. The association between work and reward exists both consciously and subconsciously. Therefore, the process of authentic reflection, advocated throughout this book, helps you consciously recognize these rewards. Rather than simply allowing these rewards to live beneath your awareness, you bring them to the forefront of your work, connecting the rewards of your incredibly difficult roles to those daily challenges. Taking the time to reflect in authentic and substantive ways allows you to access the origins of your own pathway to leadership and the rewards that guide you along the way.

The story you write in response to the "Playing for Keeps" prompt—When did you choose to pursue education as a career?—connects you to the dopamine-induced reward you experience through your work. Regardless of what spurred you to choose this profession, the values that lie beneath that choice are a foundation for the rewards you receive within it. Those same factors that influenced your decision to enter the profession initially are no less compelling now that you're in it. It's just easy to lose those connections in the full schedule and competing challenges that make up your day. To follow this through, the connective experiences between values and rewards rest in the decisions you make each day and cumulatively across your life. For example, an action such as reaching out to help a student who needs additional learning support is directly attributable to your value for personalized learning for students and the rewarding feelings you experience from that action.

By recalling the pivotal time and place described in your "Playing for Keeps" story, you can revisit the initial rewards and values of your career choice and the impact that dopamine had on your behavior. You felt compelled to act on this connection, thereby initiating your entry into the profession. Your brain constructed what you perceived to be professional experiences that would bring opportunities to experience the rewards you richly valued. You came here because you believed you would find something of great value when you arrived.

Pause for Reflection

Your life, academic, and job search experiences led you to this work. Now that you're in a school, describe your first year as an educator. What unique circumstances did you face in your first job? What were your responsibilities and your proudest moments?

The Role of Epinephrine in Stress and Motivation

The biochemical support for motivation does not end with dopamine. To broaden the context, let's look at the intricate ways your body changes and responds under stress. These reactions allow you to remain focused and engaged during those all-too-common, emotionally charged situations that comprise so much of your work. While many of the changes in your body associated with a stress reaction are initiated by a cortisol spike, focus on the more specific impact of an epinephrine release (Cleveland Clinic, 2022b). Also known as adrenaline, epinephrine is a hormone and neurotransmitter that is a part of your body's response system to a perceived danger in your environment. Your brain uses epinephrine to tell the rest of your body that it's time to prepare for a fight-or-flight response. After all, moments of epinephrine release are too common within a school environment. By connection, cortisol is a hormone produced by the adrenal glands that also impacts your stress reactions; release comes after epinephrine is produced, and it releases glucose from the liver to provide fast energy (Cleveland Clinic, 2025). For these purposes, let's focus on the impact epinephrine has on motivation.

Three ideas regarding the impact of stress on motivation are: (1) stress, and reactions to it, are a part of everyday life working in schools, (2) much attention is given to the negative impacts of frequent or prolonged exposure to stress, and (3) stress reactions are a tool to remain engaged and effective. By understanding and recognizing the changes to your body while under stress, you can leverage the positive elements to remain engaged and motivated and account for the wear and tear over time.

Epinephrine, which is produced as a normal part of a stress reaction, is important to understanding your brain's biochemistry under stress and how it impacts your motivation (Cleveland Clinic, 2022b). Epinephrine is "a chemical messenger that helps transmit nerve signals across nerve endings to another nerve cell, muscle cell or gland cell" (Cleveland Clinic, 2022b). Epinephrine release, along with norepinephrine, during a stress response affects bodily processes, including dilating your pupils, diverting blood away from digestion and reproduction toward the brain and skeletal muscles, increasing your heart rate and respiration rate, and converting stored glycogen into quickly usable glucose (Cleveland Clinic, 2022b). These effects are known as the fight-or-flight response, and they prepare your body to respond most effectively to whatever threat your mind has perceived in your environment (Cleveland Clinic, 2022b). This response is where you find the benefits of epinephrine.

The modifications that take place within your body while reacting to stress help you endure challenges and remain engaged in challenging work over the long run. Alia and Thomas Crum (2015) examine how stress can enhance your life if considered properly: "Stress has many wonderful attributes. It reminds us that we care; it connects us directly with the most challenging and important aspects of our lives." In this sense, you may regard a stressful event and your body's response to it as an indicator of your value for the outcome, as well as of the gravity of the situation. For example, if you consider a school principal having a stressful interaction with a student in crisis, the principal's body responds to sustain them through the demands of the moment while their mind recognizes the importance of handling the situation well. The principal recognizes the gravity of their interaction in supporting a student in need, and their stress response is a way for their body to perform at greater levels of strength, attention, and safety.

In the following quote, Crum and Crum (2015) continue to recontextualize the biological stress response:

> As society, we largely fail to frame stress as potentially enhancing and often miss opportunities to learn from and grow from stressful moments. That does not mean that we advocate viewing all stressors as a positive thing; but we do advocate that you embrace your stress response as a powerful tool for helping you overcome the inevitable challenges in life that can—and will—arise.

Positively reframing the stress reaction is instructional for school leaders who are surrounded by stressful events each day. Perceiving these events as being stressful indicates the importance with which you regard these events, and the physiological changes that come with a fight-or-flight activation can sustain you in trying times.

This doesn't minimize the challenges of leading schools, but further substantiates that school leaders should prioritize their physical fitness to remain healthy while experiencing stress and the impact it has on their bodies. Training for the stress of the work is a prominent theme in my previous book (Laliberte, 2025), in which I examine the impact of repeated or prolonged exposure to stress on the body in greater detail and advocate for leaders to include physiological training to prepare themselves for it as part of their professional development. Framing the stress reaction as a positive adaptation to an important element of your work will help you find a more sustainable sense of purpose over time. You know what you are fighting for, and you can prepare yourself for the accompanying experiences over time.

The benefits of your stress response do not end there. There is also a connection between stress hormones and enhanced memory, specifically relative to emotionally arousing experiences (McIntyre & Roozendaal, 2007). Science writer Isabella Backman (2023) summarizes findings of a recent study: "We actually create stronger memories when we are under stress, with cortisol helping to enhance the brain structure making them, researchers have discovered." Committing positive moments of stress to long-term memory can increase your ability to access those story elements as you seek to connect with your foundational values. For example, if you observe a student reacting in a dysregulated way to a fire drill–related alarm activation, the stress reaction you experience will imprint on your memory in such a way that you will likely recall that response prior to the next fire drill, thus allowing you to prepare the student differently for the experience. Here, the stress of the initial situation allows you to react differently in subsequent and similar situations.

If you consider retaining important memories, particularly in story form, as a key element of forming your motivation and volition, you can connect this memory enhancement directly to your functional motivation. You remember stressful events in greater detail, and that forms the foundation of what drives you.

Pause for Reflection

You always try to make the best possible decision given your capabilities and the conditions under which you make them. Yet, it is natural to look back and reconsider major decisions, especially given the challenges of your work. What are some other professional paths you might have chosen, rather than becoming an educator? What impact has this had on your life? Consider both the positive and negative elements of your decision to become an educator.

Conclusion

As with most elements of human behavior, the foundations of what you do rest in a complex interaction between your biochemical makeup, environment, and consciousness. Your actions and decisions are not as simple as you might hope. Instead, moments of decision are affected by different factors, both within your mind and body as well as from your environment. To this point, this book has looked at both the psychological foundations of actions and the brain chemistry that steers you. This complex interplay of factors operating beneath the surface of your daily behavior may seem overwhelming, but it is essential in understanding why you are motivated to act in certain ways at certain times. Trying to understand something as nuanced as motivation without acknowledging all these elements only sets you up for frustration.

With the psychological and biochemical elements now in place, turn your attention to how your personal makeup results in your motivation. Here you will find those pieces that compose your own personal motivation, volition, and the key elements of what it will take to sustain them over your career.

Telling Your Story

"Playing for Keeps" tells the story of your entry point into education as a profession. In the following space, describe the time, place, and circumstances in which you first decided to become an educator. Craft your story using the story prompt, When did you choose to pursue education as a career? (This story identifies core values that brought you to this profession.) Was this a goal you had as a young person, or did it evolve when you were an adult? What were the elements that most appealed to you?

A Dopamine Scavenger Hunt

The following is an inventory of healthy dopamine-producing activities that may form the habits and practices of your life. Check off which of these are habits for you. Then, list any dopamine-producing experiences in your life that are not on the list.

- ☐ Exercise or do other physical movement (choose from your favorite activities; Huberman, 2022; Julson, 2025; Spiller, 2024).
- ☐ Walk outdoors in environments that interest you (Spiller, 2024).
- ☐ Have a solid night's sleep (Huberman, 2022).
- ☐ Complete a project that has been nagging you or compile a to-do list and start checking off tasks (Falkowski, 2016; Spiller, 2024).
- ☐ Listen to your favorite music (Spiller, 2024).
- ☐ Identify and engage in a "quest" because humans are hard-wired to look for things (Falkowski, 2016).
- ☐ Eat less saturated fat, which research suggests may block dopamine uptake (Julson, 2025).
- ☐ Treat yourself to a favorite cup of coffee or tea—moderate caffeine (Falkowski, 2016; Huberman, 2022; Spiller, 2024).
- ☐ Increase protein intake to build up levels of tyrosine in your body, which is an amino acid that is critical to dopamine production (Falkowski, 2016; Julson 2025).
- ☐ Choose interpersonal connections instead of computer-based ones (Spiller, 2024).
- ☐ Get sunlight exposure, particularly first thing in the morning (Huberman, 2022).
- ☐ Avoid viewing bright lights between 10 p.m. and 4 a.m. (Huberman, 2022).
- ☐ Meditate (Falkowski, 2016; Julson, 2025; Spiller, 2024).
- ☐ Apply rewards to your own behavior in a random manner (Huberman, 2022).
- ☐ Interact with your pets, if you have them (Spiller, 2024).
- ☐ Create something by drawing, painting, crafting, cooking, building, and so on as you enjoy (Falkowski, 2016; Spiller, 2024).
- ☐ Spend time in (or find) a community of people where you can feel a sense of belonging, such as common interests or activities (Spiller, 2024).

References

Huberman, A. (2022, October 6). *Tools to manage dopamine and improve motivation and drive* [Blog post]. Accessed at www.hubermanlab.com/newsletter/tools-to-manage-dopamine-and-improve-motivation-and-drive on November 13, 2025.

Falkowski, G. (2016, November). Boost mood and motivation naturally with 6 dopamine kick-starters. *MS Focus Magazine*. Accessed at https://msfocus.org/Magazine/Magazine-Items/Posted/Boost-mood,-motivation-with-dopamine-kick-starters on November 12, 2025.

Julson, E. (2025, January 17). *10 best ways to increase dopamine levels naturally.* Healthline. Accessed at www.healthline.com/nutrition/how-to-increase-dopamine on November 13, 2025.

Spiller, M. (2024, December 4). Dopamine rush—27 things to do instead of scroll [Blog post]. *Excursions Magazine*. Accessed at https://sanfordbehavioralhealth.com/2024/12/04/dopamine-rush-27-things-to-do-instead-of-scroll on July 17, 2025.

List any additional dopamine-producing activities in the following space.

CHAPTER 3

Understanding the Role of Authentic Reflection

> **Coaching From the Sidelines**
>
> What caused you to accept your first leadership position? (This story identifies your call to action as a leader.) This invites you to identify the elements of your pivotal decision to become a school leader and increase awareness of your initial sources of motivation and volition. For example, you may have been inspired to lead by your interest or experience in school operations, like scheduling, or the implementation of a new instructional program.

At the center of motivation is the fundamental moment when you realize that your engagement in an activity, such as a sport, is completely optional. You are both free to join in and to walk away—with consequences given for both choices. How, then, can you come to understand your choices to join or walk away? Let's examine the world of sports, specifically the triathlon. This event combines three endurance events into a single race, such as an Ironman triathlon with a 2.4-mile swim, a 112-mile bicycle race, and 26.2-mile run held in succession with no rest between them.

Why would anyone subject themselves to this grueling event? Veteran triathlon athlete Sean Snow says:

> My main motivation is my family and inspiring them that anything we go after is truly possible, as well as my friends and all those I speak with and touch along the journey, to provide just a smother of inspiration. And having my daughter, who does them as well, is my main source of inspiration with our training days together as well as our races. I'm truly blessed for that. (personal communication, September 8, 2025)

Clearly, Snow sees his role—as an example of the power of determination and inspiration for what others can achieve—as central to his volition as an elite competitor.

For him, competition is more than a personal challenge. It is a calling and a sense of purpose in his life.

Just as in competitive sports, school leadership demands volitional clarity and being aware of your sense of purpose to fuel perseverance. There are moments that test your resolve—although in school leadership, they tend to be at certain times of the year (April) or during specific tasks (budget development). Being actively aware of your sense of purpose helps you persevere through such moments.

As of this writing, Snow continues to compete in triathlons at the age of fifty-nine. His drive is entirely intrinsic, and he stands as an example to so many who rely on the strength of their values to remain motivated in the face of a tremendous challenge.

Bringing in the subjects from the first two chapters, you can recognize the psychological and physiological elements of this level of motivation. Triathletes must have a strong intrinsic desire to compete, as well as considerable dopamine uptake to drive them. Training for such an event takes years, and then athletes must go through a substantive qualification process just to register to participate in the event. These factors explain the initial drive to enter and train for triathlons, but what about those pivotal moments in the middle of a race when competitors' bodies begin to fail? What moves these athletes to continue when even their finely conditioned bodies want to stop? It is in these moments that they need to call on more intentional and substantive reasons to continue the race.

Just like with demanding sports such as a triathlon, school leadership also places considerable demands on those who choose to pursue that career path. Physical exhaustion, cognitive overload, and the many demands of a given moment present opportunities for doubt to creep in, yet you must continue each day. The world of competitive athletes gives examples of ways you can remain inspired to persevere and prosper under these conditions. This chapter focuses on developing a personalized and substantive approach to planning for and overcoming school leadership challenges.

A pivotal factor in overcoming extreme adversity lies in a conscious awareness of the source of your motivation—what this book refers to as *volition* or the values that exist behind your decision to make a choice. Because your volition typically lives beneath your conscious awareness, it is often difficult to access when your will is thoroughly tested. By entering a position of school leadership with a clear awareness of your volition and the values that support it, you can connect with them more immediately while experiencing difficult moments.

As a school leader, the clear connection between what inspired you to enter that leadership role and the presence of those inspirational concepts in the day-to-day challenge of your work is often difficult to maintain. By developing your own approach to authentic reflection, you can sustain the connections between what you do in each busy day and the values that frame your volition. The key is to do so intentionally and regularly.

Pause for Reflection

Everyone has role models who have shaped their expectations both of leadership roles and of their own performance. Name and describe a leader you admire. It could be a person with whom you've worked or a historical figure whose actions have impacted your image of effective leadership.

Structured, Authentic Reflection and Your Motivation

Framed by an overview of both the biochemistry and psychology of motivation, let's turn to those personal elements that compose your motivation. So often, the process of reflecting on what motivates you is either undervalued or contained within some other pro forma activity. School leaders—in fact, most educators—are asked to reflect in a variety of contexts, from professional development planning processes to district workshop forms. At some point in your professional learning, you are expected to reflect on the pertinence of activities or initiatives to varying ends. For example, "For many educators, the only time they engage in reflection is when they are asked to write documents that are used to evaluate whether they should be promoted, receive a raise, or be granted tenure" (Machost & Stains, 2023). While well intended, this type of reflection can create a perception that such activities are quick tasks rather than a substantive process used to sustain your larger sense of motivation. Given the complexities of your work and how your working environment can both overwhelm and change, it makes sense to connect actively with those more authentic factors that keep you in the work. This connection requires more substantive reflection than that required on a school district form or goal-setting sheet.

Most K–12 teachers use some form of reflection, in age-appropriate contexts, to facilitate connections between existing content knowledge and new learning or as a way for students to recognize their own learning processes (UCLA Teaching and Learning Center, 2025). Given the value of reflection in the learning process in general, school leaders seldom apply it to their own work with substance or fidelity. For example, when applied to the context of professional learning, "Reflection entails considering past or present experiences, learning from the outcomes observed, and planning how to better approach similar situations in the future" (Machost & Stains, 2023). As a first step away from pro forma reflection and toward understanding your core motivations, you can reestablish reflective approaches that are committed to enhancing leadership practices and staying motivated in challenging environments. So, what does this look like in practice?

Researchers Haleigh Machost and Marilyne Stains (2023) identify three categories of reflection: (1) time-dependent (before, during, or after a pertinent event), (2) depth-oriented reflection (varies according to a progression of an element of the work), and (3) content reflections (focused on the variability of the reflection topic). These categories avoid more general reflection, such as, How did I do this year? or What will I work on next year? By structuring the scope of reflective thinking using these categories, you can arrive at deliberate outcomes that inform your actions as a leader and support changes to your work. This approach makes reflective thinking more practical. For example, a summary reflection may focus on the progression of one given school year, on the progression of leadership behaviors relative to new teachers in one's building, or on a content area, like conflict mitigation or veteran staff member evaluations. In each example, reflective thinking focuses on a targeted element of leadership behavior.

Specifically targeted toward motivation, this level of engagement also brings about more authentic ideas and an inward sense of honesty and clarity needed to understand your values, strengths, and ultimately the source of your motivation. As you begin exploring the source of your motivation, reflect on the patterns of your past decisions and what they reveal about what you value most in your work and life. Do you want to understand what causes you to choose this profession and what brings you to leadership? That begins with those stories that have shaped you—the seven stories that frame this book.

With the full and busy nature of your days, how can you take time to reflect this deeply? There is hardly time for the fundamentals of life, much less for regular, deep examination of your values. A periodic, focused, and intentional retreat can help you build time into your schedule for reflective thinking. Authentic reflection on specific circumstances of decisions and directions can reveal underlying patterns in how you think and act as a leader. It is within these patterns that you find your real values. The ability to recognize such patterns rarely comes from simple, unstructured thinking time. As mentioned earlier, begin with intentional structure to focus your thinking. Some conditions that lead to more authentic outcomes from reflection include the following.

- Establish an overall value or endorsement of the process and commit to following up on it with real opportunities to implement new ideas. For example, leadership teams can establish periodic, structured reflection time and prompts not connected to evaluation or recertification. Their stated intent is to reflect on current states of capacity and motivation.
- Find committed time away from the regular environment and rituals of your day dedicated specifically to reflection. For example, leaders can schedule brief but focused opportunities for a pulse check during their day, week, or month. These must be scheduled because if left to chance occurrences, they will not happen.
- Identify a guiding structure of inquiry that keeps you focused on the ideas related specifically to the subject matter of your reflection. This can include reflections on a given time frame, progression of behaviors, or a specific area of content. For example, leadership teams can establish a series of focused questions or prompts as a part of their goal setting for the year, which is to be completed at predetermined intervals.
- Move through the reflection process with some form of facilitation, structure, or guidance. For example, the structure of intentional reflection can be determined by the size of the school or district, the needs of the group, the experience levels of the participants, or the type of reflection needed. In some cases, personal reflection guided

by a structured process works best, though in others a facilitated group may produce more meaningful results.

- Examine outcomes from the process that will allow you to implement any pertinent results of the reflection into your work upon return. For example, while motivation-oriented reflection is best separated from the evaluation process, you can structure outcomes to tasks by asking questions such as, "Does my proposed budget reflect the instructional needs of our school?"; ask about district goals like, "Are my current priorities advancing our district's implementation of ______________?"; or question professional development, as in, "Is my participation in this post-graduate program advancing my skills as a principal?" These are all ways to be sure this reflective process supports your work and your sense of volition and purpose.

Intentional reflection is not the same as a vacation or a respite. Both are important for building and maintaining your capacity to lead effectively, but they should not be conflated with reflection and retreat as an element of leadership development. Authentic reflection as a part of maintaining your motivation is an entity entirely within itself, and it's worthy of dedicated time.

Planning for Authentic Reflection

The following elements can serve as a platform for creating an authentic reflection process for a given topic and team. (See the reproducible "Group Planning for Authentic Reflection" on page 48 for more on this topic.)

- Establish an overall value or endorsement of the process and commit to following up with real opportunities to implement new ideas.
    - Establish a comprehensive plan for the reflective process, with connections to your existing district or school structure, professional development format, strategic plan, and operational details.
- Find committed time away from the regular environment and rituals of your day dedicated specifically to reflection.
    - Establish mutually beneficial settings for this reflection based on the needs of the leaders engaged in it, as well as a scheduled time that does not detract from team members' operational responsibilities.

- Identify a guiding structure of inquiry that keeps you focused on the ideas related specifically to the topic of your reflection. This can include reflections on a given time frame, progression of behaviors, or a specific content area.
  - Articulate clear expectations for the process and outcome of the reflections, given the three areas of focus outlined by Machost and Stains (2023), reviewed earlier.
- Move through the reflection process with some form of facilitation, structure, or guidance.
  - Designate a person or team to serve as a process facilitator responsible for monitoring the time frame and adherence to tasks and schedules.
- Examine outcomes from the process that will allow you to implement any pertinent results of the reflection into your work upon return.
  - Present clear processes for following up, implementing necessary actions, establishing expectations for who is responsible, and communicating these elements with the entire team involved in the process.

Pause for Reflection

Think of leaders with whom you've worked. Who were the school leaders who most impacted your decision to lead? Who impacts your leadership practices? Remember that these impactful figures could have shaped your beliefs either through their positive example or by illustrating things that you chose not to emulate.

Now that you have established value for authentic reflection and the necessary conditions, turn to the task of supporting your motivation to lead within your school community. Given the distinction between motivation (factors that cause you to act in each situation) and volition (values and priorities that guide your actions), the first place to look for the source of your motivation is your values. If you think about what is most important to you—what you prioritize or what forms the foundation of your beliefs—you'll find a starting point for most of your choices. The concept is intuitive. You choose to act in a manner consistent with what is most important to you. Whether you prioritize concepts (like fairness) or interpersonal factors (like family), they describe what is most important to you and are at the core of the choices you make. While this thought process can become abstract very quickly, the aim is to move toward a practical approach to preserving your motivation while facing the many demands of leading schools. The reproducible "Values Inventory" (page 50) invites you to reflect on a variety of widely held values. Obviously, this is not an exhaustive list but provides focus.

Look at the connections between these values and your actions as a starting point. The foundation of most of what is important to you, your values, comes from your experiences as you grow and develop (Ponizovskiy, Grigoryan, Kühnen, & Boehnke, 2019). The concept of *value instantiation* describes the connection between abstract values and concrete behaviors. Research highlights the important role of value instantiation in bridging the gap between abstract values and specific actions (Hanel, Vione, Hahn, & Maio, 2017). In the current context, it refers to the role that your core beliefs play in shaping your actions. In other words, "Personal values are reliable cross-situational predictors of attitudes and behavior" (Ponizovskiy et al., 2019). Let's look at this in the context of school leadership.

Conclusion

Each day, school leaders make hundreds of decisions regarding the operation of the schools or districts in their care. Most decisions are procedural or contextual, yet those smaller decisions are compiled to create a school's culture. Daily habits provide insights into the leader's values and how decisions create the culture. For example, consider the degree to which a leader solicits input on operational decisions. Building use or daily schedule adaptations might be considered minor procedural decisions, yet they are also opportunities to convey the values of collective decision making and distributive leadership. By slowing down a process and soliciting genuine input from team members, the leader puts those values into action. A culture emerges from that cumulative process, bridging smaller matters and more global beliefs. It is in these larger ideas that leaders can connect to their personal values. In another example, if a leader values prioritizing caring for their family, they are likely to be more permissive with a staff member who requests time away from work to care for an ill family member. Conversely, if their values prioritize loyalty to work, a leader may be less sympathetic about that same request. Just as leaders apply these values to their professional duties, they also apply them to their conduct within the roles they occupy and ultimately to their decisions either to assume or remain in those roles.

Pause for Reflection

What factors weighed in favor of you becoming a school leader? What factors might have swayed you against choosing this path? How have these factors impacted your career satisfaction and success over time?

Many of these decisions occur beneath the surface of your awareness. This phenomenon occurs because "work intensification in recent years has complicated principals' work and made it cognitively demanding, leading to cognitive overload and fatigue, and significantly impacting their cognitive wellbeing" (Wang, 2025). Leaders sometimes accept this pace as normal and grow comfortable with the dissonance they often experience in the face of it. Therefore, it becomes even more important for you to build opportunities into your professional learning and capacity maintenance to step away and reflect on the decisions you make and the direction in which those decisions are leading your organization. This applies both to the decisions you make in daily work and to the broader matter of your presence within your role.

To cultivate this awareness, the reflective process in this book is organized around your seven stories. Within each of these stories, you can look for concrete sources of information that lead you to an accurate perception of the personal values that you carry through each day. Both through an initial examination and an ongoing awareness of these embedded values, you can carry on with challenging work with an acute awareness of what motivates you. Yes, you can make a list of what is important to you, but even the composition of that list is a subjective process. Recalling stories that describe the most formative moments in your professional experience brings an element of objectivity into the reflective thought process. This means that "previous experiences and the context influence which behaviors are considered as prominent instantiations (examples) of a value, thereby determining which values guide action in the context" (Hanel et al., 2017, p. 2). Your experiences build your values, are encoded within your mind within the context of stories, and come back to life by guiding your future decisions. Regular and ongoing authentic reflection show your values as they evolve over time and as you apply them to your daily work with intention rather than as subconscious side effects. Therefore, you know why you are doing everything you do because your actions are consistently aligned with what is most important to you.

By taking the time to bring these values to your conscious thoughts, you can approach those most difficult decisions with a renewed sense of clarity and certainty. For example, if you value personal dignity and respect, this may influence how you approach difficult conversations with staff members who require redirection or corrective action. Through authentic reflection, you become consciously aware of what matters to you, and with that comes a clearer answer to the questions that accompany our most challenging times: Why do I do this? Why do I accept the challenges and demands of leading schools? For example, you may come up with any of the following responses: "Because I believe in creating opportunities for students," "Because a personalized approach is most important to me," and "Because leading schools affords me that opportunity." Your responses will obviously be your own, but what would that look like? Fill in the blanks for these sentence stems.

- Because I believe in ____________
- Because ____________ is most important to me
- Because of ____________ and ____________

With a clear sense of purpose and a focus on those things that matter most to us, we are inspired to persevere in greater challenges.

Telling Your Story

Focus on your decision to enter the leadership element of education in the story prompt "Coaching From the Sidelines." Identify the elements of this pivotal decision as the initial source of your motivation and volition. What caused you to accept your first leadership position? (This is your call to action as a leader.)

Group Planning for Authentic Reflection

The following questions are intended to guide your building or district team, which is charged with planning reflective activities, in an authentic and meaningful way. These topics refer to structural components of reflective activities that are indexed specifically to your organization and connect your work to ongoing initiatives or priorities.

- Establish an overall value or endorsement of the process and commit to following up on that process with real opportunities to implement new ideas.
  - How will participants be introduced to the expectations of this reflective process?
  - How will this process be connected to your existing systems or expectations?
  - How will outcomes from this process be recorded, get communicated with all stakeholders, and receive adequate follow-up, wherever appropriate?
- Find committed time away from the regular environment and rituals of your day dedicated specifically to reflection.
  - Where will this activity take place? How is this environment conducive to deep reflective thinking and meaningful dialogue?
  - How will the environment be structured to ensure appropriate focus and attention?
  - How will the group address distractions, emergencies, or a need to alter the schedule?
- Identify a guiding structure of inquiry that keeps you focused on the ideas related specifically to the topic of your reflection. This can include reflections on a given time frame, progression of behaviors, or a specific content area.
  - How will the time be structured to maximize attention required for each task or element?
  - How will norms or expectations for participation be developed and communicated?
- Move through the reflection process with some form of facilitation, structure, or guidance.
  - Who will be responsible for maintaining the guiding structure?
  - How will a facilitator, timekeeper, or process monitor be identified or retained?

- Examine outcomes from the process that will allow you to implement any pertinent results of the reflection into your work upon return.
  - What expectations have been established for outcomes or products of the reflective activity? Will input be sought from within the group or other stakeholders?
  - How will responsibility be delegated for communication, documentation, or follow-up from reflective outcomes? What documentation will be expected?

Values Inventory

The following list of values has been compiled from a variety of sources as a starting point for discussion and reflection. Review each value and rate them according to your own level of priority for that value. You may wish to add other values at the end, with your own level of priority for each. Please remember; not everything can be a high priority!

Value	High Priority	Focus	Awareness	Low Priority
Integrity				
Autonomy				
Courage				
Belonging				
Well-being				
Creativity				
Fulfillment				
Family				
Freedom				
Self-improvement				
Independence				
Honesty				
Loyalty				
Ambition				
Work Ethic				
Professionalism				
Wisdom				

page 1 of 2

Other values not included in this exercise but that you find to be of value:

CHAPTER 4

Dealing with Shifting Motivations

> **Reassessing Your Playbook**
>
> What are the three most important achievements of your overall career thus far? (This story describes core values and how they change over the arc of your life.) This comparative exercise asks you to examine a larger body of memories to recognize how your values may have changed over time. As you move through life, your priorities change with your circumstances, and volition shifts as well. Entering a committed relationship is one such example. Where once you may have prioritized work or your own personal needs, a relationship can change the way you allocate your time and resources. Being aware of these shifts is key to remaining connected to what motivates you.

One of the most challenging elements in the life of an athlete is the passage of time. In childhood and adolescence, athletic performance is often limited by physical immaturity (Saville, 2025). Therefore, optimal performance must wait until a period where size, speed, strength, and skill match competition demands. There is an ideal window during which athletes' bodies are primed for high-level competition. As athletes physically mature, their abilities become more evident within the structure of the sport (Albaladejo-Saura, Vaquero-Cristóbal, González-Gálvez, & Esparza-Ros, 2021).

Seasoned athletes know that as the demands of a sport take their toll on their bodies, the arc of their performance inevitably declines. At first, when "older" athletes continue to compete, they rely on advanced tactical knowledge, interpersonal skills, technique, and leadership abilities to remain at their respective levels of competitiveness. As time and the cumulative impact of their sport continue to affect their bodies, athletes learn to rely on their minds to a greater degree. Eventually, they may either seek out opportunities to compete at less intense levels or in other sports, or they may put their considerable experience and knowledge to work coaching others. Some choose to walk away from competition altogether, choosing instead to pursue other facets of life, including leadership positions in their places of employment (Stones, 2020).

Regardless of the path they choose, athletes must accept the changes that come and adapt. There is no pre-prescribed curve. Athletes learn to rely on external metrics for performance and their internal drive to know when it is time to make a change.

Here lies a pivotal connection between sports and leadership. As school leaders gain experience and wisdom as years pass, the work becomes smoother. However, leaders experience negative impacts over time as well, such as physical or cognitive aging, the compounding of adverse experiences, or even the environment changing around them. Leaders aren't the same after twenty-five years as they were in, say, their fifth year of work. Just as athletes evolve their conditioning and playing styles, leaders remain aware of how they are changing and evolving over time. For example, leaders may still have the motivation to lead, although in a different role or place, or they may recognize it's time to step away from leadership. This chapter looks at different elements of that transition and at how awareness of these factors can supplement the desire to preserve motivation and volition. Just as athletes must adjust their approach over time, educational leaders can adapt the way they approach their work as they grow and change. This kind of awareness and adaptation is central to remaining motivated over the arc of your career.

Pause for Reflection

You move forward by identifying sources of affirmation that you value in your professional advancement. What were some of the earliest moments of personal recognition or professional affirmation within your work experiences? These experiences can help you identify those parts of your work that you found to be most affirming at that time. For example, earlier in your career you may have valued professional awards, but as you grew, you came to prioritize personal achievements.

Changing Values With Changing Life Experiences

Your values are shaped over time as you have different experiences and progress through life. Significant life events bring new priorities—for example, a school leader may think about their work in all new ways if they become a parent or experience a life-altering illness. Suddenly, priorities are challenged, and thinking shifts. Experiences within your role as a leader combine with other experiences to bring about entirely new perspectives. To ignore the arc of these experiences is to remain blind to those core values that form the basis of your professional decision-making process. As you grow and accumulate experiences, your volition will change along with what you value. Those changes provide, yet again, more value for the practice of ongoing and authentic reflection to maintain intentional self-awareness, as discussed throughout this book. Leaders grow and change as time passes, which gives value to the ability to recognize and adapt to changes. To understand this phenomenon better, consider the developmental stages of adulthood.

Psychologist Erik Erikson (1950) developed the *stages of psychosocial development*, which is "a lifespan model of development, emphasizing how social relationships shape our sense of self" (McLeod, 2025). This chapter only explores the final three stages of his model, which are directly related to adulthood (Orenstein & Kaur, 2022).

1. The young adulthood stage (ages 19–29) examines the development of intimacy versus isolation.
2. The middle age stage (ages 30–64) confronts the matter of generativity versus stagnation.
3. The old age stage (65+) extends the balance of integrity versus despair.

Now, you'll examine each stage in greater detail.

In the young adulthood stage, people struggle with relationships with those who accompany them on life's journey (Orenstein & Kaur, 2022). If you are alone, the motivational factors behind your actions are likely based on your own self-interest. You are compelled by what you think is best. If, however, you choose to engage in a relationship, another value enters the equation. You now must consider your partner as well. Your volition has changed with the expectations of this relationship. Naturally, the degree and nature of that change is relative to your beliefs about how best to conduct yourself in a relationship, but all the same, the equation is different. The addition of children, a blended family, or an extended family with relatives forming a household together brings additional factors to consider and elements that alter motivation. You are no longer accountable only to yourself—you consider other lives in your decisions (Orenstein & Kaur, 2022).

Relative to your work as a school leader, such a change in your life introduces a conflict specifically in how you allocate your time. There are significant schedule demands that come with assuming a school leadership position that may be easier to answer when your life is focused just on work. Complications arise when you find yourself conflicted between school events and those associated with your family or relationship. For example, you may find yourself conflicted between attending a drama production at your school and a different event in which your child may be participating. This situation demands a clear perspective on your values.

Middle age includes most of people's working lives. Here, Erikson identifies a conflict between generativity and stagnation (Orenstein & Kaur, 2022). *Generativity* is "a concern for people besides self and family that usually develops during middle age" (Generativity, n.d.). *Stagnation* is "a state or condition marked by lack of flow, movement, or development" (Stagnation, n.d.). Some people choose to focus their attention on a smaller group, whether on themselves, their relationship, or their immediate family. People choosing this path develop different scopes of thought, and different volitions relative to their life choices.

As far as your work as a school leader is concerned, your awareness of these conflicts and how they play out daily can support a more intentional approach to the work and ultimately support your desire to remain motivated and fulfilled over time. To illustrate this point in a concrete way, a generative approach to your work might involve active steps to support the next generation of leaders by mentoring up-and-coming administrators, actively volunteering in the community, or even coaching youth sports. Applying the concepts behind this element of Erikson's work can help you recognize that such actions not only support causes in your community but also help you avoid feeling stagnated and disillusioned with the demands of your work. They help you as much as they help your community.

In old age, Erikson examines the balance of integrity versus despair (Orenstein & Kaur, 2022). The conflict for those over sixty-five is pertinent to how many school leaders choose to end their careers. Here, there is a description of a common degree of dignity and a perception of one's value in the scope of their life, particularly when considered at the end of one's career when paired with retirement. A person with integrity experiences a sense of completeness or value for their work when they look back at their career. In pursuit of this sense of accomplishment, many school leaders may be motivated to choose paths that result in the long-term preservation of their work or of a succession of leadership extending beyond their tenure. The values behind their actions indicate the importance of this sense of completeness.

Therefore, this sense of completeness explains why so many leaders find activities that preserve their legacy fulfilling as they approach the end of their working years. Naturally, each leader has a different set of circumstances that govern their ability to build that legacy. In some situations, leaders can groom their own replacement, or they may be able to support and promote the development of subordinates who demonstrate potential to take on leadership positions in the future. Additionally, a retiring leader may be recognized with different forms of affirmation, such as an award or having something named for them that recognizes their contributions. Chances are you will find any opportunity to pass on leadership skills and opportunities to be highly rewarding.

Pause for Reflection

Most people are motivated by looking forward in time and constructing hopes and expectations for themselves. What are three aspirations that you have for your future as an educational leader?

As you grow as a person, the values and priorities that guide your decision making change over time. Simply put, what motivates you today will likely change tomorrow. Framing your daily work using ideas supported by your developmental stage will allow you to intentionally build both an overall approach and a specific schedule that supports your needs. As discussed, there is a natural process to the development of adults that brings about different needs at different times of your life. By paying attention to these needs, you will be able to grow within the challenges of the work of school leadership. Over time, this supports both maintaining your capacity to lead effectively and remaining motivated.

Remaining Aware of Your Development Over Time

Engaging in substantive reflection is best approached in regular intervals over a year and with a different focus at pivotal events in your life. This is an intentional way to reassess your personal playbook in a meaningful and approachable way and ensures you remain aware and engaged, regardless of the circumstances challenging your sense of motivation. So, how often would you need to engage in this kind of periodic, deep reflection to remain self-aware and motivated? Naturally, the cyclical nature of a school year lends itself to annual reflection and adjustment; although, if you adhere to the type of focus mentioned earlier in this book, that reflection will be more focused on role-specific matters and daily functioning as school leaders. However, a different level of focus becomes useful regarding the impact of significant life events or developmental changes.

What sorts of events might necessitate a deeper examination? The following lists four times when you will benefit from deeper reflection on professional circumstances that can change your perspective on your role and your approaches within it.

1. Significant life events, such as entering a long-term, committed relationship, the purchase of a home, or the birth of a child
2. Hallmark personal moments, such as the arrival of a zero (decade) birthday, a geographic relocation, or the completion of a long-term goal like a graduate program
3. Personal tragedy, such as experiencing the loss of a loved one
4. A negative life-altering event, such as the end of a long-term relationship or a natural disaster

Ultimately, you must evaluate the significance of such events and weigh the impact these events have on your priorities and values. Too often, people compartmentalize these types of events and assume they have little impact on professional motivation. As with most things, it is better to turn your attention toward it and determine the level of impact than to simply assume and later find yourself struggling or wondering. By building in a purposeful examination of significant life events, you can account for their impact on how you think about your role as a school leader. To help with this, The Social Readjustment Rating Scale (also known as the Holmes-Rahe Life Stress Inventory) offers an extensive list of the most stressful and disruptive life events that people can encounter, along with a point value for each that weighs the severity of the event (Holmes & Rahe, 1967). This exercise can be used to identify impactful events that may provide you with opportunities to reflect on your core values and any resulting changes in your volition and motivation. (Visit www.dartmouth.edu/eap/library/lifechangestresstest.pdf to access an online version of this scale.)

The key to reflecting on these life-altering events is committing to a meaningful, structured process with an openness to positive outcomes. Steps to structuring such a process include the following.

1. Define the event or milestone.
2. Explore your own responses to and feelings about this event—both in the positive and the negative sense. Here, as always, honesty is crucial.
3. Anticipate the many potential impacts that this event may have on your day-to-day life, as well as your values and priorities.
4. Consider a deliberate series of outcomes focused on future decision making, both within the professional and the personal spaces.

The timing and structure of this kind of reflective thinking are personal. The only requirements of authenticity are that you commit to participating fully, you engage in the process in a timeline that supports potential outcomes, and you implement specific outcomes based on what you discover in the process. Also helpful to this process, the reproducible "Values Changing Over Time" (page 62) will assist you in reflecting on how your values change over time.

Pause for Reflection

Think deeply about the affirmations and positive reinforcements that you have encountered relative to becoming an educational leader. What recognitions or encouragements have inspired you to persevere? Identify a pivotal moment that affirmed your choice of profession. These moments of recognition can indicate both the sources of affirmation that are most meaningful to you and the subjects of that affirmation, such as the distinction between professional awards and personal recognitions. You can learn much about your values from the sources of affirmation that mean the most to you.

Conclusion

Recognizing how life events can change both what motivates your work and the underlying values that shape your volition are pivotal to remaining motivated despite challenges. Both the passage of time and the occurrence of significant life events impact your motivation. As in many other components of this work, ongoing awareness of how these elements impact your decision making relies on regular, authentic reflection and the willingness to consider changes that you will encounter over time. Minimizing or ignoring these connections leaves yourself vulnerable to their impact beneath the conscious surface of your awareness. By recognizing the changes that occur across the scope of your lifetime, you can stay connected to your authentic sense of purpose and the true source of your motivation.

Telling Your Story

Broaden your focus a bit here as you use valued experiences from your past to construct motivational support for your future. The story prompt, "Reassessing Your Playbook," asks you to examine a larger body of memories to clarify those that were most formative in your development as a leader, particularly over time.

Craft your story using the story prompt, What are your three most important achievements of your overall career? (This story helps describe core values and how they change over the arc of your life.)

Values Changing Over Time

While many educational leaders try to maintain a distance between their personal and professional lives, encountering significant events that impact your value systems, and ultimately your volition, is unavoidable. The following protocol for reflecting on significant life events gives leaders in these situations a process to guide their reflection and subsequent ways that their motivation or volition may be impacted. This protocol is intended to be a guide and may be modified as necessary to accommodate the specific requirements of an event.

- ***Step 1:*** Describe the event and any necessary details required to understand it. Try to focus on telling the story of the event itself without expanding on your own opinions or feelings.

- ***Step 2:*** Compose a bulleted list of the different observations, thoughts, or feelings that you've encountered because of this event. Again, focus on describing your reactions rather than justifying or analyzing them.
  -
  -
  -
- ***Step 3:*** Look at the list from step 2. Which of those observations, thoughts, or feelings did you find to be the most disruptive or uncomfortable? List those in the following space with a brief description for each part that made you feel unsettled.
  -
  -
  -
- ***Step 4:*** Of those experiences identified in step 3, which relate directly to your priorities or values relative to your role as a school leader? List those and include a brief note for each on the relationship between the event and your role.
  -
  -
  -

- ***Step 5:*** Compose a list including each element that you described in step 4 and identify how they might change the ways you make professional decisions, both relative to how you conduct your work and in your motivation and volition to carry on as a school leader.
  -
  -
  -
- ***Step 6:*** Compose resolutions that will guide you going forward following this significant event, keeping in mind the impact it has had on your priorities and values. These resolutions should be as specific as possible, even including examples of situations that would require you to invoke them. For example, you may resolve to establish a rotation of coverage for evening events that will allow you to be more present for your family. Include these resolutions in your personal journal or display them somewhere prominent as a reminder of their importance going forward.

In the weeks and months that follow this reflective activity, it may be necessary to revisit these resolutions or the process that produced them and modify them as needed. Intervals can be specific to the resolution. For example, if you resolve to be more present at family events, the interval could be structured around your child's sports season or drama production. It is most important that they remain accurate and authentic as your perceptions of this event shift over time.

CHAPTER 5

Coping When Work Feels Too Heavy

> **Leaning Into Your Team**
>
> Can you identify a time when you were extremely upset by a situation that violated your ethics or professional boundaries on the job? (This story identifies your passions and principles and helps you understand where your ethical lines are.) There are moments when school leaders find themselves frustrated or disillusioned. You may find your capacity diminished even to a point where you would benefit from outside support. Recall a moment that pushed you to the brink of frustration. Perhaps you even contemplated walking away altogether. What can you learn from this experience?

Athletes, from the youngest ages, learn customs, traditions, and social mores that accompany their given sport. For example, at the end of a game, young baseball players line up and shake hands with the other team. Golfers are silent when others are about to strike the ball. In several sports, tournament participants sometimes trade team pins with opponents. These traditions exist independently of a sport's rules or requirements, yet they are passed on to teach young athletes the value of politeness, sportsmanship, or the recognition of a greater connection beyond sports. Athletes grow up knowing that their participation exists within a larger context of fairness and humanity. As athletes grow and advance in each sport, they learn that sometimes they simply do some things because they are right and are expected within positive participation.

Similar ethics and customs exist within your work as a school leader; although, they are not always as clearly defined or universally adhered to. Sometimes those unwritten rules are local or regional, and other times they are held across the profession. For example, regional groups of school leaders often adhere to a "no poaching of teachers" agreement during the summer. It is also customary for schools or districts to share counseling staff during tragedies. These traditions illustrate overarching values within school leadership that transcend logistics. They reveal value for colleagues within the profession and recognize the interconnected nature of the larger community in which everyone operates. With that value, you'll find a collective source of will that influences your decision to become and to remain a school leader.

This collective will describes a sense of community within the educational leadership profession that often goes underappreciated or unused as a resource for individuals who may find themselves struggling with diminished capacity of many kinds. By inviting you to lean into your team, seeking support from your colleagues within your school or district, and in the broader profession, becomes intentional. You can recognize the potential resources and supports present throughout the school leadership profession and use them to preserve and build on your personal capacity to lead. This requires the humility to recognize your own boundaries as well as a willingness to reach out to others as professional and personal resources. You do so not as an act of weakness but as an acknowledgment of the collective strength of this professional community.

Pause for Reflection

Often, you experience frustration when your expectations of a certain situation are not met. If you recognize these expectations ahead of time, you are better able to remain aware of how they impact your reactions. Identify or recall some of your earliest moments of overall frustration with some element of the profession. What frustrates you?

Leadership Capacity

Leading schools is more than a job choice. It involves assuming a highly visible and demanding position within a community and often results in a loss of personal privacy and space that most people take for granted. This is a part of school leadership, but it can wear you down over time and contribute to feelings of depletion and frustration. Every leader has a personalized ability to function under job stress and demands given their health, disposition, and experience. In my first book (Laliberte, 2025), I distinguished this ability by referring to it as your *leadership capacity* or your physical, cognitive, emotional, and motivational threshold for enduring the demands of the work. By considering all possible variables that impact your job performance, you can maintain this capacity to perform at the outer limits of your personal abilities, or your composite skills, abilities, and experience. This practice leaves you with a broader perspective on the different ways you can act to sustain both your capacity and motivation.

There are many different approaches to actively maintain your leadership capacity (Laliberte, 2025). This chapter establishes the connection between your capacity and the support available from the broader profession for an individual practitioner who may be struggling. There are many elements of leadership capacity that are within your control, such as sleep quality, appropriate nutrition, or social and emotional supports for school leaders. Given those elements, there are also unique times when you, as a school leader, may experience fatigue or frustration that, though typical of the work, requires some form of external intervention. Here, those collaborative elements of the profession may serve as a resource for maintaining your capacity to lead. Accessing resources such as professional mentoring or coaching may be appropriate in some situations, or the camaraderie of an issue-specific group or network of other school leaders may work in others (such as a support group for new administrators or a collaborative group of leaders working together to solve challenges in rural districts).

So, how can you know when to turn to your network of support? Although your colleagues are a source of support during trying times, over-relying on them can wear them thin because they also carry a heavy load. All school leaders struggle with diminished capacity at one time or another, and most worry about becoming a burden to their colleagues. Here, once again, authentic reflection and self-awareness take center stage. By developing an ongoing awareness of your leadership capacity and of the resources available to you, you will be able to distinguish between needing to pay greater attention to what comprises your personal capacity and when it is time to ask for help.

Pause for Reflection

Building off the idea of expectations, look ahead with more specificity at the areas of your work that mean the most to you. Name a challenge within education that you would like to solve or improve over the course of your career.

Support From Within the Profession

The community of school leaders and their collegial support influences your volition and, ultimately, your career choices. Most experienced school leaders can cite many examples of when they were lifted by a colleague during a trying time. Leaders are a source of understanding and support for one another because they understand the challenges in this work.

The community of school leaders surrounding you can be the glue that holds your work together. For you to be able to access this peer support, you must first define it in context. *Peer support* is more than just a supportive comment or commiseration. In some circumstances, it begins with the intercession of a mentor who might support your advancement within leadership circles. In others, that support may come from the structure of your position or state of your career, such as the promise of future advancement or succession. In any case, there is a source of professional support in your relationships with other colleagues or mentors.

This support often varies greatly between districts of different sizes, locations, available economic support, and ideological framework. Given this potential disparity in opportunities that support your capacity maintenance, each school leader is responsible for familiarizing themselves with those available resources, either on a local, regional, or national level. Understanding these resources is fundamental for developing a plan to actively manage your leadership capacity.

Qualities of a Supportive Community

Within the leadership community, you will find certain concepts and axioms that form a support system for advancing quality candidates into school leadership and sustaining them once they're there. The following is a list of the most predominant factors—although it is not an exhaustive list, it does indicate some of the supports you may have. Some of these thoughts are regionally or positionally specific, while others are more prominent in different generations of leaders. The goal here is to recognize those unwritten rules you may expect yourself to adhere to or to ignore. They become a part of the equation that inspires you to lead.

- **Professional duty, succession, and obligation:** These factors can be more prominent sources of expectations for early-career school leaders. Educators recognize the strength of their own ideas, and they pair them with an ethic within schools that recognizes the importance of leadership progression. For schools to thrive, there must always be a next generation of leaders in the making. School leadership is not for everyone, but maintaining a pipeline of capable leaders is crucial to maintaining the quality of learning experiences for our students. Do you see yourself in this pipeline? For example, a veteran principal recognizes a teacher's leadership potential in the school building. The principal encourages and nurtures that teacher through a graduate certification program and the beginning of their leadership career, as well as serving as a source of support as the leader advances.
- **Personal loyalty:** Building from the preceding item, many practicing leaders see growing future leaders as central to their professional competence. This ethic, and the personal relationships that form between mentors and mentees, often results in school leaders entering the profession at the urging and support of those administrators who see potential in them. This is the concept behind a now common practice of succession planning in school leadership. The result can build a sense of duty or obligation both to the profession and to the mentor. Are there other leaders who have encouraged or mentored you, to whom you feel personal loyalty? For example, while working with their regional school leadership association, an early-career superintendent develops a friendship with a veteran superintendent in another district. They discover common beliefs and challenges and become a source of support for one another.
- **Postponement of outcomes:** Some school leaders see their role as a temporary means to some larger goal, whether financial or positional. They accept a role to attain a more desirable one later. This could be an ascending aspiration, such as a person becoming

an assistant principal as a step toward a principalship. It could also be a veteran teacher accepting an administrative position to increase the security of their retirement. In either case, this means agreeing to do something now to attain something better later. Have you ever accepted a position as a means to another end? For example, an emerging school leader aspires to someday serve as a systems leader in a larger district. Realizing the importance of breadth of experience, the leader chooses to serve as a principal in a challenging school district both as a means of making a difference in that community and of preparing themselves for future success as a systems leader.

- **Expectation of advancement:** In some leadership environments, there is an inferred expectation that a leader will "move up" within a given amount of time. This could range from an assistant principal becoming a principal or a building administrator transitioning to a district or systems level. This differs from the previous idea that advancement itself is expected. Leaders advance because it is what they are supposed to do. Have you ever moved up in a position because you felt like it was time to do so? For example, an assistant principal realizes that, after four to five years on the job, they are ready to step into a principalship of their own. They seek out advice and support from their current principal as well as others currently in the role.
- **Family or social expectations:** Some leaders may feel compelled to choose a path to leadership based on the expectations of some member of their family or social group. Whether to follow in the footsteps of a family member or to meet an expectation of attainment, the leader chooses to pursue this path motivated by the expectations of someone close to them. By attaining the approval of a loved one or to receive some measure of affirmation, the decision to advance comes from a perceived reward or recognition for moving up. Do you recognize or perceive the expectations of someone close to you as a factor in your decision to lead? For example, as a member of a family with two or three generations of school leadership, a young teacher is inspired to pursue a leadership position by the examples set by their family.

While these factors are often specific to the circumstances of an individual leader, most experience some form of these as they move into and through the world of school leadership. They form elements of support for leaders that are specific to the profession. Most are extrinsic motivational factors with connections to intrinsic values. For example, if you look at personal loyalty as a motivating factor, you'll find the extrinsic influence of a mentor or supportive colleague. Acknowledging that, you must also intrinsically value that person's support and approval for their encouragement to take root and motivate you to act. In that way, what seems to be an extrinsic influence is connected to your own intrinsic values.

Pause for Reflection

Look at your work within a school day and identify an expectation of yours that often isn't met. Describe a hot button issue, a general principle, or recurring situation that frustrates you, such as disrespect, lack of effort, and so on.

In each of the five social expectations, you must consider a larger context of support from a professional community of educational leaders. Whether these factors influence your motivation or not is a personal and relative matter—yet they still exist. Like most professions, these social rules contribute to the advancement and development of the next generation of school leaders. They are not written expectations, and they are neither universally held nor adhered to. They are, however, elements of motivation for many school leaders in the profession, and they constitute an element of volition. The degree of their influence is, once again, a matter of personal insight.

Like with so many different elements of motivation, there is the importance of accurate self-awareness. If you can recognize your own thought patterns and how they impact your decision making, you will be better able to harness them as a source of motivation. For example, if you know that you have accepted a principalship partially motivated by professional obligations and the expectations of a valued mentor, you will have additional fuel to continue in that challenging role. Leaders also benefit from an additional element of support. Perhaps, if you are feeling frustrated or questioning your motivation to continue, you might be reinspired by setting aside time for a conversation with a mentor or with other school principals who share your level of commitment to those professional obligations. To simply dismiss such thoughts without acknowledging them gives doubt a chance to fester and wear away at your motivation beneath the surface of your consciousness. It is why leaders have those moments when working on a tropical island seems feasible.

Sources of Support Beyond the Profession

Naturally, there are situations where, to maintain the capacity to lead, you will have to turn to resources outside of the community of school leaders. There are more obvious situations such as your physical health and the necessity of working with appropriate doctors. However, other circumstances may feel more awkward for you as a leader, although they are certainly no less crucial in the interest of your well-being and capacity. For example, substance abuse counseling or treating mental health conditions may be uncomfortable for a school leader aspiring to project strength and stability to their constituents, even though either situation represents a considerable challenge to your capacity. Such situations demand your humility to recognize how they impact your capacity to work at the outer limits of your abilities, as well as your willingness to serve as a role model to others who may be confronting similar challenges. Your willingness to acknowledge your struggles and to confront them in an active way serve as notable examples for healthy living and your prioritization of your leadership responsibilities over any part of your ego that may intercede.

As you develop a broader understanding of what impacts your leadership capacity, you will realize the importance of seeking out appropriate supports for those variables, regardless of whether they are within your personal control; appropriate elements for collegial support and collaboration; or appropriate challenges that require you to step outside your role for the support of qualified resources in the broader world. Ultimately, your aim is to work at the outer limits of your capacity to lead in the best interest of your students, staff, and community.

Conclusion

The professional communities in which school leaders learn and grow provide considerable support to aspiring leaders and those well experienced in the profession. This is particularly important when leaders find themselves teetering at the edge of burnout and struggling to connect with a source of volition that they may not be able to see. (For help, see the reproducible, "Rating Scale for Stressful Events or Ethical Dilemmas" on page 74.) Within these relationships, leaders find shared values and ethics that can be a source of support during difficult times, as well as a positive element of motivation to keep them working at optimal levels within their roles.

Telling Your Story

Was there a time that you were extremely upset by a situation that violated your ethics or professional boundaries on the job? (This prompt identifies your passions and principles.) Where are your ethical lines? There are moments when school leaders find themselves frustrated or disillusioned. You may find your capacity diminished to a point where you would benefit from outside support. Recall those moments from your experience thus far that pushed you to the brink of frustration. Perhaps you even contemplated walking away altogether. What can you learn from this?

Rating Scale for Stressful Events or Ethical Dilemmas

The challenges of leading schools come from an accumulation of individual events leading to a more generalized stress load. To navigate this environment, leaders must develop an active awareness of those elements of daily work that they find engaging versus those that they feel are stressful. This rating scale allows leaders to examine typical areas of challenge along a continuum of positive to negative stress. By clarifying this distinction within the scope of their experiences, leaders can develop strategies for adapting to the negative elements of stress they encounter daily.

Academic Challenges					
Concentration	**Dread**	**Discomfort**	**Indifference**	**Engaged**	**Energized**
You receive a call from a parent challenging their child's final term grade.	1	2	3	4	5
A student raises an objection to the validity or viability of a book assigned by their teacher.	1	2	3	4	5
A student in your school demonstrates a level of skill and knowledge beyond your existing mathematics program. The parents request to meet with you to discuss alternatives.	1	2	3	4	5
In examining your assessment scores, you discover a significant need for intervention in a grade level. You have no budget to add programs, but these students need help.	1	2	3	4	5
Behavioral Challenges					
Concentration	**Dread**	**Discomfort**	**Indifference**	**Engaged**	**Energized**
You are called to address a belligerent student who is refusing to leave a classroom.	1	2	3	4	5
Students stage a walk out to protest a new school board policy.	1	2	3	4	5
A fight breaks out between students in the cafeteria. You are short-staffed with administrators that day.	1	2	3	4	5
You receive word that a significant number of students are failing due to high absenteeism. You must respond within the next twenty-four hours.	1	2	3	4	5

Human Resources Challenges					
Concentration	**Dread**	**Discomfort**	**Indifference**	**Engaged**	**Energized**
A staff member does not report to school on time, leaving their responsibilities uncovered.	1	2	3	4	5
A support staff member has been taken into police custody during non-work hours.	1	2	3	4	5
A staff member resigns three weeks into the school year. They give you no notice of their departure.	1	2	3	4	5
Due to a conflict in scheduling a professional development event, you discover that you do not have adequate staff to supervise students during lunch. The bell rings in fifteen minutes.	1	2	3	4	5
School Management Challenges					
Concentration	**Dread**	**Discomfort**	**Indifference**	**Engaged**	**Energized**
Three days before the school year begins, you receive word that an influx of students will require you to reconfigure your schedule significantly.	1	2	3	4	5
An outbreak of sickness among support staff leaves your building short of appropriate classroom support for high-needs students. You must compose a short-term plan to respond.	1	2	3	4	5
As the school year starts, your teachers report that they are short on mandatory textbooks. You have no money left in your textbook account.	1	2	3	4	5
An extreme driver shortage renders your transportation provider unable to staff the bus routes. They don't know how long it will take to complete all routes.	1	2	3	4	5
Safety and Security Challenges					
Concentration	**Dread**	**Discomfort**	**Indifference**	**Engaged**	**Energized**
You are responding to a report of an unidentified adult who has gained access to the building.	1	2	3	4	5
A fire alarm sounds just as students are entering the building in the morning. It's raining profusely.	1	2	3	4	5

During a routine evacuation drill, your staff discovers that there are three students missing from their classes. The fire department has not removed them as part of the drill.	1	2	3	4	5
Just as the bell rings for students to exit your building for recess (or dismissal), you receive a frantic call from duty staff that a bear has been sighted on school grounds.	1	2	3	4	5
Legal and Policy Challenges					
Concentration	**Dread**	**Discomfort**	**Indifference**	**Engaged**	**Energized**
You receive a phone call from an attorney requesting a meeting with them and their clients, a family in your school, to discuss a matter regarding a cocurricular activity.	1	2	3	4	5
You are advised by your school board chair that you will be implementing a new student dress code when the school year starts in two weeks.	1	2	3	4	5
You have received word from your governing body that you have just three weeks to implement a new mandatory grading system in your school.	1	2	3	4	5
A community group reaches out to you to file a formal objection to the content of a book that is taught in your school.	1	2	3	4	5
Public Relations Challenges					
Concentration	**Dread**	**Discomfort**	**Indifference**	**Engaged**	**Energized**
As you are preparing to dismiss students for the day, you are informed that a group of adults are forming a protest line outside of your main entrance. You do not know the subject of their protest.	1	2	3	4	5
A local TV station reporter arrives in your office with a camera crew and asks if they can interview you about a disciplinary matter that has been reported to them by a community member.	1	2	3	4	5
You have twenty minutes to compose an email to parents regarding a controversial incident in your school.	1	2	3	4	5
You have been asked to deliver a speech at a national conference to a group of 5,000 of your fellow school leaders.	1	2	3	4	5

Major Weather or Environmental Incidents					
Concentration	**Dread**	**Discomfort**	**Indifference**	**Engaged**	**Energized**
A significant storm front is moving in while school is still in session. You must facilitate an early dismissal.	1	2	3	4	5
A weather emergency has resulted in power outages and school cancellation for what is expected to be at least two weeks. You have four hours to compose a response plan.	1	2	3	4	5
Your school experiences a water system malfunction—you have no water. You have ninety minutes to get it fixed or facilitate a dismissal.	1	2	3	4	5
While investigating a series of student and staff illnesses, you discover the presence of mold between the walls in a wing of your building.	1	2	3	4	5

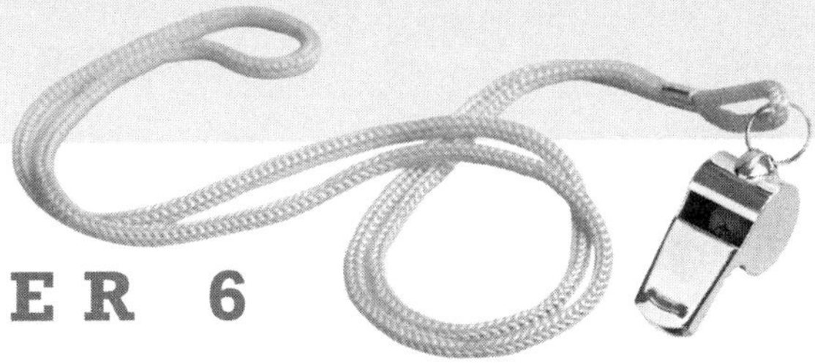

CHAPTER 6

Deciding to Stay or Go

Changing Teams

What would cause you to walk away from your profession? (This story identifies areas relative to sustaining yourself within the profession.) For example, some leaders find themselves conflicted over regulatory requirements or district policies requiring them to conduct themselves in a way that is not consistent with their beliefs, such as a change in academic standards or student behavioral expectations. Here, you are asked to consider issues that challenge the core of your volition and beliefs.

In collegiate and professional sports, where there were times when restrictive rules and logistics tied a player to a particular team, there are now mechanisms in both that allow players to change teams with far more flexibility. Free agency allows professional athletes to change teams at the end of their contract, and collegiate athletes in the United States can change schools in a similar manner (NCSA College Recruiting, 2026). Any sports fan recognizes that the transience of talent is now an institutionalized part of sport. It is acceptable, and at times encouraged, for an athlete to transfer to another team or organization to find a better fit for their skill set. While some sports fans see this as institutionalized disloyalty, others recognize the value of an orderly approach to relocation. Ultimately, the practice recognizes the changing nature of team needs and roles for athletes within them. Environments evolve over time, as do the requirements of individuals within them.

In this context, no value judgment is attached to the idea of changing organizations; instead, it is regarded as an illustration of a fundamental element of educational leadership. Your ability to lead successfully often depends on your placement in a position and organization where your skills are needed and your values are shared. Like athletes, the circumstances in schools or districts evolve over time, and the requirements of leadership change with it. Where you may have been a fit upon your initial appointment, these changes may necessitate your movement either to different roles or different organizations, or maybe a change in your life—or a change you're seeking, such as moving to a new area—dictates the need for a professional change as well. Whatever the reason, the goal is to stay in an environment where you can be as effective as possible for as long as possible, in the best interests of both students and staff.

This chapter acknowledges the transient elements of school leadership and examines the distinction between when to persevere and when to leave. The ability to see, in accurate context, whether your window of effectiveness has passed with changing circumstances is central to effective leadership. Are you still the best person to lead this school or district? Does the school or district maximize your abilities and contributions? Is it time for a change? There is no shame in an accurate assessment of these questions. Just as in sports, the portability of leaders' skills and experiences has become a part of the work, which demands an intentional approach, which you will explore in this chapter.

Pause for Reflection

Everyone has a breaking point. Being aware of these limitations can prepare you to respond appropriately, either by seeking support or reevaluating your position. Have you ever questioned remaining in education as a profession? Why did you stay? What core issue caused your frustration?

How to Know When It's Time To Move

While much of this book is dedicated to identifying and maintaining motivation to lead in schools, there are times when a healthy and motivated leader recognizes new conditions that may inspire a change. For example, there is a clear difference between a situation that requires grit and perseverance and one where conditions have rendered the leader no longer a fit for the environment (or vice versa). That difference is found in the match between the skills and values required of leadership in an organization, and the same skills and values that a leader brings to their work.

Circumstances and the demands of school leaders evolve over time in school communities. For example, if a school is implementing a new instructional program, their leader is required to bring a working knowledge of curriculum and instruction to support it. If a school faces a budget crisis, fiscal management is required as a leadership strength. Not all leaders are strong in all areas, which is where there may be potential incongruities. An incongruity is the absence of a match between leader and role. It is not a sign of an unmotivated leader but one still engaged in their work who has some disconnect between their strengths and the demands of their position. It's time to do something different, but what? Where? When?

Effective leadership depends on your fit within the environment in which you lead. Demands and expectations vary according to the community you serve, and often, challenges in specific environments require an emphasis on specific skills. A key element of effective leadership is remaining aware of how you align with these expectations and being able to discern between a professional challenge and a sign that it's time to make a change.

All school leaders, from assistant principals to superintendents, rely on the compatibility of their skill sets, experiences, and values to determine their effectiveness in their roles. Recognizing discrepancies in those areas may be a call for a change in environment, if not an overall role. There may also be times when the deliberation is much deeper and permanent—that you may no longer have the capacity to serve as a leader in schools at all, and that either a job change or retirement is the best course of action. Ultimately, this determination is at the heart of any deliberation regarding leadership. Leaders are called to recognize whether they are in the right role and in the right place.

Pause for Reflection

Building off the last reflection, turn your focus toward the future in anticipation. Looking ahead hypothetically, is there an issue, situation, or principle over which you would quit your current job?

Naturally, any deliberation on this matter highly relies on your life circumstances. Most education leaders in their thirties do not have the financial stability to consider retirement, but they could consider a job change or a step away from school leadership. Prior to determining any future action, deeply examine your fit within your current role. This determination requires self-awareness and a willingness to confront potentially awkward truths about your current situation. Still, your match within your current role is the starting point for considering a change. The alternative is a random series of career changes in pursuit of what you perceive to be a more advantageous situation. Begin where you are because the decision whether to make a change at all usually precedes deciding the nature of the change. The following questions can help you reflect on your current role and situation.

1. What was it that drew you to this role in the first place?
2. What expectations did you bring to your work at the beginning?
3. How have those expectations come to fruition? Have they been met, or have they changed?
4. What are the most significant contributions that you've made in your role to date?
5. What goals do you have for the next year, three years, and five years?
6. What is your greatest source of frustration in your current role?
7. If you could change one thing to reduce this frustration, what would it be?

By focusing your attention on the specifics of your current role, you can clarify the exact source of your frustration and the degree to which you can operate within that environment and change these frustrating matters.

Signs It's Time for a Change

An early-career school principal finds themself amid a jam-packed schedule at the end of a school year. The principal is exhausted and overscheduled, though still working to greet students and staff with a smile each day. While reviewing morning emails, the principal receives a job posting for a nearby school that is higher paying and less of a commute. The principal may be tempted to seek out a new situation because of extrinsic factors and current level of exhaustion, but doing so may also be detrimental to both their current leadership capacity and long-term career effectiveness. While a new job may be appealing given their current state of mind, a change also requires leaders to reestablish credibility, gain familiarity with new systems and people, and orient themselves to a new set of expectations and challenges. Changing jobs is sometimes necessary, but it is not always as easy as it seems. Is it time for the principal to consider a change or time to focus intently on their current role and how their execution of that position impacts capacity? The principal will arrive at a clearer answer through reflection and analysis of their current performance level.

Often, leaders see typical frustrations as signs that it's time to change positions. However, this is not necessarily the case, particularly if you form that opinion at a time of year or in a state of mind when your capacity has been diminished by your demanding work. For example, at the end of a school year or amid budget season may not be ideal times for evaluating your viability within a position. Instead, you can gain deeper and more accurate insights by engaging in this focus after you've had a chance to put some distance between you and that stress, such as during the summer or between school years. Thus, your capacity to make life-altering decisions becomes much more reliable. Another way to help decide whether to stay in your role or position is self-evaluation.

Once again, this is part of the focus on authentic reflection, but it is also an intended element of your professional evaluation process and goal setting so you can maintain your capacity to lead effectively. These systematized elements of gauging your performance serve a purpose to your supervisors, but they are also an opportunity for you to step back and see yourself within your role and circumstances. Should you benefit from a reflective prompt to direct your thinking, you will find the reproducible "Role Change Reflection" on page 89.

Performance Assessment

Naturally, you can assess your performance anecdotally or through the lens of your existing professional evaluation model. Both can be helpful; although, you may not have the time and context at your disposal to complete such a process. The following steps can help school leaders identify ways to engage in a more timely and informal approach. Author Matt Gavin (2019) advises leaders to address self-evaluation by including the following four elements.

1. Complete a self-assessment using external measures of your performance.
2. Observe yourself by using video to engage in critical self-evaluation.
3. Ask for feedback to identify discrepancies between self-perception and the perceptions of others you lead.

4. Build and maintain a robust network to develop trusted relationships as a source of guidance, coaching, and advice.

These four elements are quite like the components of a standard school leader evaluation system, regardless of the format. Each of these four elements invites you to turn your focus within to understand both the quality of your daily work within your leadership role and your broader compatibility with the role itself. Using these steps, you'll learn what you do well versus what needs improvement, and you can reflect regularly on your fit in a role or circumstance. The structural elements may feel forced or contrived, but they can also help you step outside of the emotional elements of this process. No one likes to feel like they aren't doing well in their current role, yet everyone needs this objective point of view to obtain a clear perspective, independent of their biases about their current job performance. The results will inform your decision regarding whether you should continue in your current role or make a change.

Having gathered as much information about your work within the current role, next turn your attention to how that information aligns with your job expectations. This information about job expectations can be acquired through a formal analysis of role descriptions, conversations with immediate supervisors or colleagues, or your observations regarding the role and how it has changed over time. For example, if you garner information that identifies curriculum planning as an area of relative strength, but you see that your district has concluded an implementation cycle, you might consider that an incongruity with the role. Similarly, if your school is about to begin a major building project, but you have no experience or knowledge of this process, the same conclusion would be reasonable. An accurate and comprehensive perception of how you are experiencing a leadership role can help you build an understanding and engage in the next step in evaluating your place in a role. You can look at the leadership expectations of the role itself.

Pause for Reflection

The community of school leaders can be a source of support to colleagues who might be struggling with motivation and a sense of purpose. What advice would you offer to a fellow educator who is contemplating leaving the profession?

How to Tell if Your Role and Circumstances Fit You

Having developed a clear understanding of your ongoing performance in your current role, you now have the necessary information to tell whether you should consider continuing in that role. Although this component of the decision-making process can be emotionally charged, turn to objective information as much as possible. For the purposes of clarity, this consideration divides into several categories: (1) the role and its circumstances, (2) enjoyment of the role versus resolution of its key responsibilities, and (3) facing opposition in the role and knowing when to stay.

The Role and Its Circumstances

The role refers to the conventions and expectations of the job in the operational (day-to-day) and situational (big picture) sense. For example, if the demands of a person's life preclude them from participating in evening activities, a principal or superintendent position may not be advisable. Both roles include the operational expectation that the leader attends many evening events, meetings, or community activities. It's just part of the job. In another example, if a leader is averse to reading long documents, they may not want to pursue roles that require knowledge of legislation or policy development for a particular situation.

These examples may seem to be common sense, but school leaders regularly remain in roles over time, knowing they are averse to, or avoid altogether, required elements of their jobs. Leaders may put up with some job requirements to stay in roles where they enjoy other requirements, but this can wear on them over time. These elements will change over time, necessitating ongoing awareness of the role. By examining your relationship with these requirements on a regular basis, you can remain aware of your status within them and the required level of motivation to continue completing parts of your role that you don't enjoy or in which you are not as effective.

The circumstances surrounding a given role are more specific to the setting in which a person works. As stated earlier, in some circumstances, a school principal may be expected to be present at many community events and functions. However, in other circumstances, there is less expectation of principals in the wider community. Instead, their focus is more intent on the operation of the school itself and any cocurricular elements of the instructional program. These expectations are often specific to a given community and evolve over many years and different administrations. It is not unusual for these roles to be different in neighboring communities, making it even more important for school leaders to be aware of them as early as possible during the initial hiring process. Because these expectations are widely held, they seldom change and are often an element of public perception relative to the leader's job performance.

By remaining aware of the expectations of the role and the circumstances in which you work, you will be better able to assess your fit as a leader in a particular community. This awareness helps you determine what comes next.

If you need to apply some additional structure to your thinking about your role as an educational leader, the reproducible "Motivational Reflection" (page 91) will facilitate a closer reflection regarding your current role and your expectations of it.

Enjoyment Versus Resolution of Responsibilities

Determinations about role fit and role circumstances are separate from your enjoyment of a role, which is no less important than the other considerations. There are parts of most people's work that they do not enjoy, yet leaders are challenged to remain motivated and engaged to stay effective. Taking a realistic look at the impact of positive and negative job elements can also give insight into your larger job satisfaction. Keep in mind that "being happy at work and loving what you do is an overall productivity booster and enhances performance. People who enjoy their jobs are more likely to be optimistic, motivated, learn faster, make fewer mistakes, and better business decisions" (USC Dornsife, 2023). In other words, being actively aware of your satisfaction relative to the responsibilities of your role is important for staying motivated.

Not all school leaders step away from the job because of dissatisfaction or burnout. Sometimes, the work in a role has simply concluded, and it is time to move forward with another challenge. Former school principal Matthew Ebert describes his decision to make a professional change in this way:

> There was nothing left for me to do, but there would always be more work to do. For that growth to occur, I had to get out of the way. That was how I could best take care of my colleagues, my students, and myself. (Ebert, 2024)

While this mindset may seem different from what's typical of disillusioned leaders, it is common within the profession. If you consider how frequently school leaders are hired for their specific strengths relevant to a given school, it's not unusual that a leader may feel compelled to move on once those needs have been addressed.

For example, there is a specific set of needs and knowledge required to guide a school or district through a major building project. These circumstances require a fluent knowledge of funding, logistics, scheduling, and building and infrastructure details, just to name a few. Leaders are often hired specifically because they have demonstrated competence in these areas. Given that focus, a leader may feel both a sense of accomplishment and a compulsion to move on to new challenges when that project has concluded. Similar things could be said of schools or districts facing major instructional initiatives or staffing challenges.

Opposition and When to Stay

Of course, circumstances exist within the leadership space where your continuation within a role is either restricted or outright opposed by someone in an influential position who does not support your presence. This could be a supervisor, a school board or committee member, a prominent community member, or any other person who may be able to influence your day-to-day work within a role. This calls for a different element in a reflective process. You must consider the degree of impact that this person has on your effectiveness within the role, as well as the cost of their opposition relevant to your personal leadership capacity. Clearly, you likely would not leave a role because of one person, but when considering your level of frustration with the role, you might need to look closely at the cost of working around this person each day. In this manner, the person becomes a variable in a larger equation—not a causal factor. To fully understand your current situation, consider all factors that impact your work.

Then, there is the ever-present possibility that reflecting on your current role could yield a totally different conclusion—that it is best for you to stay. Remaining open to this possibility, even in the presence of considerable discomfort, lends authenticity to the reflective process. You must be open to all possible outcomes, including this one. Engaging in a thorough process of reflecting on a decision to remain or leave your role should not be considered a failure or a waste of time if you decide to stay. Much to the contrary, this sort of thinking is deeply affirmational and can provide you with important insights that clarify your place in the current role and affirm many elements of your volition in making the choice to stay. As established earlier, leaders come to work with a clear understanding of why they are there. When you ask yourself why you do what you do, you will have an answer readily available.

Conclusion

Ultimately, the process of discernment regarding your current leadership role is a part of your work and an expectation of your ongoing role as a leader. Schools are cyclical by nature. Each school year represents a punctuation mark in the lifespan of both the students you educate and in the operations of your school. By taking an active and reflective approach to your presence in a role, you assure yourself that you are the right leader for your school or district, and this is the right school or district for your leadership skills. This is a fundamental element of leading schools with authenticity and purpose.

Telling Your Story

The story prompt for "Changing Teams" helps you bring together the material and reflections of this chapter to see the distinction between embedded job stresses and more decisive signs that it may be time for you to make a change. As you analyze your current situation, identify the key challenges or areas of your work that require your attention relative to sustaining yourself within the profession. Craft your story for the prompt, What would cause you to walk away from your profession? (Describe potential pain points in the work.)

Role Change Reflection

Use the following reflective prompts to supplement your existing evaluation and reflection systems in developing a clearer sense of where you are in your current career and whether it could be time to consider a change.

- Reflect on your expectations of your current role.
- Are your expectations being met? Are they in the process of being met?
- Rate your level of satisfaction from 1–5 with 5 being the highest. ________
- Rate your optimism level from 1–5. ________
- Rate the quality of your working environment from 1–5. ________
- What are your aspirations for next year?
- What are your aspirations for the next three years?
- What are your aspirations for the next five years?

- What are your aspirations for the next ten years?

- Outline your path from your current role to your five-year aspiration.

- Consider your expected role and the environment in which you work. Do you want to move up where you are versus moving somewhere else?

Motivational Reflection

The following reflective activity directs your thinking during times of frustration or when you are experiencing conflicted thinking regarding your current position. You should consider the following prompts when you have time away from your work to reflect in a deeper manner. It is also recommended that you complete your responses in writing to compose your thoughts in a clearer and more substantive manner.

- What has motivated you to act in some of the more memorable or significant events in your lifetime? How can understanding the sources of past motivation inform your future decisions?

- Prior to making any kind of change, you must first understand the root cause of your disillusionment in your present role. Reflect on your current level of performance within your role

- If a change is needed, what kind of change will best fit you in your current circumstances? Same role, new place? Different role, same place? Different role, different place? A radical change outside of your current sphere?

CHAPTER 7

Sustaining Your Motivation

Hanging the Championship Banner

What are the most fulfilling rewards of your work? (This story identifies the outcomes that you value most and the priorities behind them.) Refocus on the positive elements of your role as a school leader. For example, you may have found yourself drawn to school leadership to have a more active role in developing innovative instructional programs but are unable to do so as a principal due to the logistic demands of your role. Is there a way for you to reorder your priorities to take a more active role in developing new instructional initiatives?

A desire to win becomes actual victory through daily habits, such as how an athlete studies game videos to reflect on past performance relative to expectations and sets ambitious goals for performance improvement. There are few places where you will find a more prolific use of statistics, measurables, and means of quantifying performance than in the sports world. Athletes' bodies are measured, the details of their physical abilities are quantified, and each perceivable detail of their performance within the sport is broken down and monitored.

Although school leaders don't need to develop as many measurement tools as those for athletes, the concept of measuring performance is instructional to accomplish a similar end—to take a broad concept (for example, becoming a better hitter in baseball) and develop a means of improving elements of it (for example, improving contact ratio, hitting for power, increasing on-base percentage, and so on). By considering your work as an accumulation of skills and knowledge, you can then focus on analyzing areas that best offer opportunities for improvement. This is true of the tangible parts of the work, such as knowledge of law and policy, as well as of the more abstract skills, like being a more empathetic listener. The evaluation of many of these elements lies in external evaluation of one's own performance along with the associated outcomes.

As a school leader, you are likely not a stranger to assessment. You evaluate student performance to understand the effectiveness of academic programs and instruction, and you regard elements of student care through measuring attendance, truancy, disciplinary actions, and other indicators of student well-being. These data sources correlate with performance through the external variables they measure. However, what about internal matters, such as your job satisfaction, professional capacity, or underlying motivation? Variables related to these are often beneath conscious perception, which is why authentic reflection is so helpful. The challenge here is to formulate an approach to help you put this reflection into practice.

The starting point for authentic reflection lies in a more directed focus on specific parts of your performance as opposed to general perceptions or aspirations. Focus on the details to develop a practical and concrete approach to this work. This chapter will bring together all the material from previous chapters and formulate the elements of your personalized plan for sustained motivation. The idea is to give concrete and actionable form to authentic reflection. In many cases, the planning tools that follow create a common starting point for developing specific goals, as well as defined measures for attaining them. This creates a common approach to your process but maintains a personalized outcome that is uniquely yours. Whether structuring a retreat experience for your team or establishing your own independent practice, authenticity remains the goal.

Pause for Reflection

An important element for building sustainable strategies to maintain your motivation is the conscious awareness of rewards in your work. Describe a moment when you felt a complete sense of fulfillment by a reward as an educator. How about outside of work?

The Quest for Authenticity

As you focus on the details of sustaining your motivation within the demands of school leadership, consider authentic experiences, which are those connected directly to your own personality, goals, and volition. They support your understanding of your role and your experiences as a school leader. They are meaningful to you beyond what your professional development program or evaluation system requires. Authentic experiences transcend some of the simple procedures and activities that comprise many systems of documenting professional development and create a deeper clarity and specific context for your daily work.

Your efforts to remain motivated, regardless of what form they take, must produce authentic results and implementable outcomes. Broad understandings and goals are helpful to frame this work, but the process cannot end there. Ultimately, motivation is not a collective act because entire teams are not motivated at the same time. Instead, a team is a collection of motivated individuals who share a common set of values and goals at the same time. For example, beginning with a broad statement, such as, "We believe all students can learn," is a great way to frame a discussion; although, the power of such a statement rests in the planning and implementation of programs that follow it. A school community can only broaden the effectiveness of *all* student learning if it plans and implements a system of supports, deploys adaptable curricula, and advances assessments that accommodate varying methods of demonstrated learning. You can advance the broader goal by building components of a system that support that goal.

Each team member charged with enacting these broad values must have the opportunity to reflect on them in an authentic way so they can evaluate their own degree of commitment to the values. Such statements must be authentically held among the individual members of the group to gain traction because, too often, these sorts of statements are considered as givens. However, once they are more intensely scrutinized, they are found to be qualified or incompletely accepted. Therefore, this scrutiny is the starting point for authenticity.

The reproducibles "Planning Guide for Time Away From Work" (page 106), "Building Characteristic Environments for Authentic Reflection" (page 107), and "Retreat Planning Template" (page 109) are designed to help individual leaders and leadership teams engage in authentic reflection that will build capacity, improve both individual and organizational performance, and support leaders in sustaining their connections to what motivates them.

The success of the results rests in the following.

- The ability to focus inwardly on specific values and components of your performance as a school or district leader, regardless of whether these elements are positive or negative
- The willingness to move beyond surface-level responses and into deeper causes or outcomes
- The commitment to develop actionable outcomes from this reflection and a plan to implement them
- The acceptance of possible discomfort, either through realizations within yourself or in conversations within your team
- A value for the process of examining the details of your behavior, why you choose specific values, and what this says about your motivation

By committing to authenticity, you open yourself to the positive possibilities that come with deliberate reflection, but you also expose yourself to possible realizations that bring awkwardness or even the impetus to change. For example, you could realize that you are steps away from being an outstanding school principal or that it is time to change jobs or careers. You may have to challenge your foundational beliefs in the face of changes in your life or in your family. You also may uncover truths about yourself that could place you at odds with valued colleagues or comfortable situations. In any case, your goal is an honest and authentic understanding of all that motivates your choices. The resulting clarity becomes the foundation of your sustainable motivation, regardless of the direction in which it brings you.

Pause for Reflection

You can look to a broader world in your efforts to build sustainable strategies to stay motivated within your work. What people, events, or situations do you find to be inspirational as an educator and as a leader? Where do you look for these stories or inspirations? In what ways might you expand your exposure to these inspirations?

In developing an actionable approach to sustain your motivation, this chapter divides the work into two parts: (1) the four seasons of motivational maintenance and (2) strategies for troubleshooting. We'll begin with the four seasons of motivational maintenance.

The Four Seasons of Motivational Maintenance

Schools exist in cyclical patterns defined by a school year. Rather than allowing the ebbs and flows to derail how motivated you feel in your work, you are better served to build around them. You can implement good ideas only for them to fail because they were implemented at the wrong time of year. School years are incredibly full, and often, you can find yourself trying to sneak in tasks during times of the year that aren't conducive to that particular work. For example, practicing school leaders know the end of the school year is busy, so they race to make it through assessments and curricula; address complex logistic issues, such as placement or the following year's schedule; hire new staff while honoring outgoing ones; and try to find time to wrap up their own professional development efforts while setting the table for the next year.

The resulting atmosphere is certainly not conducive to authentic reflection, but many districts require leaders to write end-of-year reflections or attend leadership retreats. This isn't a shortcoming; it's a result of a too-packed schedule and a more pragmatic experience of reflection within your work. So, what would a school year look like if you approached it differently? What would a reflection schedule look like if it was built around the realities of the school environment? Again, look at the cyclical nature of athletic competition seasons, which mirror the cyclical nature of a school year as seen in the following list.

- Preseason (summer, planning)
  - Retreat and reflect.
  - Plan for the long term, contingencies, and logistics of implementation.
- In-season (fall, operationalize the plan)
  - Focus attention on the operation.
  - Build check-ins for plan elements.
  - Use periodic capacity checks and reflection.

- Postseason (spring, troubleshooting and adaptation)
  - Collect necessary data.
  - Plan transitions.
- Offseason (reflect, recover, and adjust)
  - Plan for respite and recovery.
  - Take care of personal health and well-being.
  - Take a vacation.

This cyclical approach to task development frees up leadership teams to engage in work that otherwise may fall off their schedule but may save them both time and headaches in the long run. One such task is *contingency planning* or, as it is referred to in sports, *adjustment planning*. This anticipatory activity can ensure that leaders are prepared for potential challenges throughout the school year and reduce the inherent stress of adjusting to circumstances on the fly. Challenges include logistics problems, emergency operations planning, and so on.

Among the core ideas behind this overview is the practical realization that leaders must always be prepared to adjust to those unforeseen issues or emergencies that are a part of leading schools. Ideally, the year would pass without them, yet it rarely does. Some districts plan for these events by including a "goal" in their yearly planning process. In other words, they examine and evaluate those elements of their yearly goals that they are willing to modify or postpone if there is a significant disruption to their school operations, as was seen during the COVID-19 pandemic in 2020. This event wasn't something that very many school districts had anticipated, but those that had some form of response plan were able to implement strategies more quickly and with greater fidelity to their guiding values. Therefore, if leaders plan for unforeseen complications and allow the space and time to adjust to them, they enter a school year prepared with both the resources and mindset to correct the course, if needed. This approach minimizes the disruption of these incidents within leaders' minds and the broader school atmosphere.

The cyclical approach that follows is not unusual for many school districts, yet the intentional structuring of reflective time is rare. By building elements in schools to accommodate life's daily demands, leaders can preserve space and time to engage in a more authentic approach to reflective thinking. This practice sets the tone for the rest of the planning, both in the long range and operational scopes.

Planning in the Preseason

This component begins in the summer after the offseason from the previous year ends. School leaders emerge from the offseason as energized and refreshed as possible, ready to engage in authentic reflection. This is not to suggest that time off fixes everything; although, with some intentional planning, this downtime can be used for respite and recovery. Having had some time to decompress and rest, school leaders have the headspace to engage in deeper thinking. Therefore, the preseason is the time for planning and engagement. It is optimal that any retreat planned be organized as a facilitated opportunity to look internally at a leader's performance and status and focus on what comes next. As clarified in the "Retreat Planning Template" reproducible (page 109), a structured and broadly focused retreat experience connects operational details to the broader context of district goals and vision—not focused on logistics. Clarity of that retreat's purpose is crucial to authentic reflection. If the purpose of the gathering is to look at organizational procedures, policy, or logistics planning, call it a meeting—not a retreat.

A sample task may include formal retreat experiences, either for leadership teams or for individuals, in a manner consistent with the "Retreat Planning Template." Also, other structured or facilitated planning activities or professional learning experiences should be focused on district goals or initiatives. This is also a great time for group-building experiences for administrative teams.

Most educators experience some form of a retreat in their careers, but are those experiences conducive to deep and authentic reflection? There is a continuum of retreat experiences that range from unstructured quiet time to what is, in effect, an extended administrative team meeting. We attach no value judgment to retreats falling anywhere along this range; however, the term *retreat* usually indicates intentional approach to reflection and introspection. Therefore, whatever a retreat looks like within an organization, it should bring participants to that purpose.

Retreats are not glamorous vacations or cushy getaways. They are highly focused events designed to allow leaders the time and space to engage in meaningful reflection and planning for the upcoming school year, unencumbered by the demands of their regular work environments. By taking the time to establish the value of retreats, you can preempt any minimizing comments or criticisms from within your team or from the broader communities you serve.

While there are no rigid formats that will be most effective everywhere, some elements can guide your thinking when structuring reflective experiences. The goal is to take time away to think deeply about the significance of past events, present circumstances, and future goals. This includes removing stigmas associated with retreats or reflection time. Don't joke about it or minimize it. The intention here is to facilitate professional growth, preserve motivation, and stay connected to your sense of purpose. Characteristic environments for authentic reflection include the following.

- Intentionally structure the time and environment for reflection.
- Plan in advance to remove potential distractions or stressors. Have what you need on hand to allow for the time and head space.
- Use structured activities to facilitate engagement and use stories to structure your thoughts.
- Use methods of recording outcomes, values, or changes resulting from the reflection experience.
- Have expectations for outcomes, including a means of following up on plans across the coming school year.

The reproducible "Building Characteristic Environments for Authentic Reflection" (page 107) can be used to develop strategies for including these environments in your professional development plans, and it will bring a clearer process and purpose to the planning and execution of a substantive, authentic leadership retreat for your school or district.

Operationalizing During the Season

Once the school year begins in the fall, the start of the season, things become much more practical and operational by design. Guided by the outcomes of the summer reflection and subsequent goal setting and planning, leaders can put into practice the concepts that they have developed through their reflections. The focus shifts to practical and pragmatic matters once students arrive. Just as with a sports season, leaders prepare for a long and difficult grind, and they anticipate the challenges that will lie ahead. They are prepared to adjust their plans to meet the requirements of their daily challenges as needed.

A sample task may include consultations or meetings with operational teams within buildings or districts that are highly focused and task oriented. Problem-solving sessions may center on such challenges as facility operations, emergency response planning, or budget development. Individual pulse-check meetings between systems- and building-level leaders may focus on capacity and well-being.

Troubleshooting and Adapting in the Postseason

During spring, the school year is beginning to wind down. Logistics challenges and the demands of daily work have eroded some of those ideas that leaders worked so hard to develop at the start of the year. This postseason slump is anticipated and is a part of the reality of leading in schools. Schools are complicated and rely on many different people in varying roles for ongoing success. The human factor brings with it complex interactions and complications. Through regularly scheduled check-ins, leaders can evaluate what worked, what didn't, and what remains within the confines of the school year. However, there isn't time to step away from the daily grind to engage in these status checks, so these check-ins are brief and scheduled as close as possible to school operations. Take time out within the busyness to evaluate and adapt where possible and acknowledge anything that must be postponed. Leaders also collect qualitative and quantitative data that can be used later for subsequent reflection and planning.

A sample task may include solution sessions focused on the evaluation of specific issues, such as student behavior, attendance concerns, implementation of a specific instructional initiative, or a wider challenge to the school or district (funding crises, staff shortages, scheduling challenges, and so on).

Reflecting, Recovering, and Adjusting in the Offseason

Most school environments feature some form of break around summer. This can offer school leaders the opportunity to schedule time for personal respite as well as for retreats and reflection. Ideally, these two things occur in this order; most leaders do not have the capacity to engage in deep reflection when they are exhausted from the school year. By recognizing the importance of active recovery and rest, leaders prepare themselves to restart the whole process—to return at full leadership capacity during the next preseason, ready to engage once again in the process of authentic reflection. They restore their motivation and reconnect with the deeper ideas behind our volition.

A sample task may include structured out-of-office time, including administrative coverage for incidental needs or issues, travel to locations beyond communication range, planned experiences away from the work environment, or engagement in special interest projects you may have outside of work. The following includes some more ideas to help you develop personalized resources that support your reflective activities or individual retreat materials.

- Adhere to daily habits that remind you of why you choose this path. Strategies for building intentional awareness of the source of your volition include:
  - Visual reminders, such as photos, books or mementos for display
  - Affirmations or daily readings
  - Reflective time, prayer, or meditation
  - Personal check-ins or connections with valued colleagues or mentors
- Personalize your experience by focusing on what you need to maintain your capacity in the following areas.
  - Physical and physiological conditions
  - Cognitive and mental conditions
  - Emotional status with appropriate supports
- Use strategies, such as the following, for troubleshooting perceived times of low motivation. Develop an individual plan for those times when you just don't feel connected or motivated anymore.
  - Establish a go-to person and reach out to them, using consultations, conversations, or a wellness check.
  - Consult an inventory of variables affecting your frame of mind to identify elements of life that may negatively impact your motivation. Include physical conditions, interpersonal relationships, stress responses, emotional support, and extraneous or non-work-related matters.
  - Plan an intentional break in routine within the structure of your workday. Reschedule other commitments to spend more time with students, participate in outdoor activities, or engage in content that you enjoy.

By using this approach to the four seasons of motivational maintenance, leaders will become more comfortable with honest introspection and difficult conversations among colleagues and have greater consistency in the values that motivate them to do their work over challenging days and successive years.

Pause for Reflection

You can leverage the cyclical nature of your profession to your advantage in maintaining and renewing your motivation to lead. What are some of the recurring events within the school year that you look forward to most in your current role?

Strategies for Troubleshooting

While a collective retreat is a great way to bring together a team of individuals around a common purpose, there are times and situations when you feel the weight of your work, and with it, you experience motivational low points. This book has addressed many of the practical elements of staying motivated, connecting with your values, and identifying the stories that have defined you so you can control your environment to increase the biological and psychological elements of your motivation. At this point, let's look at what that can look like in practice. The following list includes practical activities that you can use in down moments to remain connected with your sense of motivation. Not all elements are for everyone, but there is something here for most people. Feel free to add your own ideas to the following list of activities that support motivational maintenance.

- Create time in your schedule for physical exercise or favorite creative activities.
- Use intentional structuring opportunities to share stories with colleagues or to reconnect with former colleagues, mentors, or friends.
- Clear out any impediments to good sleep hygiene so you can get enough quality sleep.

- Practice any kind of meditation, prayer, or intentional reflection that brings you value. This includes spending time outdoors, even when it is difficult to structure.
- Add decorative elements to your workspace that remind you of the people, places, ideas, or things that are of greatest value to you.

This list could go on at great length if it included all your personal experiences, yet the intention of the list is to remind you of some common starting points. Hopefully, you have either been reminded of motivational exercises that you miss, or you have been inspired to remember some other activity of restorative value to you. As always, the path to preserving motivation is a personal one, and you begin with common elements to build out more personal pieces.

Conclusion

In the broader scope, remaining motivated to lead in the complex and demanding atmosphere of schools is too important to be left to your subconscious awareness. By bringing your motivation and volition to the surface, you allow yourself to connect with them on an ongoing basis. Building a commitment to ongoing and authentic reflection only serves to strengthen this connection. The strength of these ideas can power you and inspire you through those difficult moments you face each day. When a moment arises that leaves you wondering "Why do I do this?," you will find the answers close at hand.

Telling Your Story

You increase your access to affirming elements of your work by remaining aware and surrounded by the people, ideas, and experiences that represent the positives in what you do. By structuring authentic opportunities to reflect on the positive impacts of your work, you can see the meaning and value in even the most challenging tasks you face. Craft your story using the prompt, What are the most fulfilling rewards of your work? Identify the outcomes that are of greatest value to you and the priorities that exist behind them by refocusing on the positive elements of your role as a school leader.

Planning Guide for Time Away From Work

School leaders will often take time away from work only to find that time interrupted. This results from a lack of planning for contingencies and redundant responsibilities. This is an important element of establishing opportunities for respite. Before planning, it's important to understand the intended nature of your time away from work. Then, use the following planner to preserve greater purpose from your next time away from work.

- **Vacation:** Time dedicated to experiences, travel, family, and friends (active time, not work related)
- **Respite:** Time dedicated intentionally to rest and recovery (passive time away from work where you focus on rest, recovery, and health)
- **Retreat:** Time dedicated to key elements of work—time spent away from work (active time, work related, structured, and task-focused in a non-work setting and schedule)

Duration of time: ________________

Focus of time: ________________

Add accommodations for contingencies in your building or district for continuation of operations in your absence.

Contact person: ________________

Expectations for communication with you (that is, your availability by email, text, or phone): ________________

Ongoing projects or matters to be addressed while you are away:

Anticipated return time and date:

Contingencies in case of a delayed return:

Building Characteristic Environments for Authentic Reflection

The following tool is intended for your use in structuring reflective time differently in your professional development programming. The goal is to take time away to think deeply about the significance of past events, present circumstances, and future goals. Remove the stigmas associated with retreats or reflection time. Don't joke about it or minimize it. The intention here is professional growth to preserve motivation and stay connected to your sense of purpose.

- Intentional structuring of the time and environment with the stated purpose for reflection
    - **Dedicated time of predetermined length:** When will time be added for reflective activities?
    - **A quiet setting free from distractions and other tasks:** Where will reflective activities take place?
- Advanced planning to remove potential distractions or stressors—have what you need on hand to allow for the time and head space
    - **Necessary materials on hand for writing, music, and so on:** List any needed materials for the planned activities.
    - **Predetermined use of technology needed for the format:** List any technology needs.
    - **Meals, drinks, bathroom access, and so on (prearranged):** Attach a comprehensive schedule for any activities, including accommodations for these needs.
- Structured activities to facilitate engagement—use stories to structure your thoughts
    - **Determine the format and the desired outcomes of your reflection ahead of time and develop prompts:** Identify desired outcomes with references to any prompts, reading, or necessary affiliated materials.

- **Collect necessary data or resources to bring to the task—avoids having to stop your thoughts and go looking for things:** List data to be collected with persons responsible for collecting it and expected format.

- Methods of recording outcomes, values, or changes resulting from the reflection experience
    - **Include goal-setting formats or templates from your respective school or district:** Reflective time should produce actionable outcomes. Reference any required formats and attach needed templates or materials.
    - **Develop action steps with responsible parties, as well as a plan for communication and follow-up:** Attach any articulated formats for these outcomes, along with the people responsible for communication.

Retreat Planning Template

A structured approach for building out a district retreat is needed that optimizes the opportunities that come with a meaningful program (versus either a vacation or a two- to three-day meeting that is sometimes called a retreat).

The following template is intended to guide district administrators in planning and executing an effective and meaningful retreat experience for building administrators. It identifies important components of retreat planning and ensures that anyone planning such a retreat has an opportunity to consider the full scope of developing one. Not all elements will apply to every retreat, but with this planning tool, you will be able to consider which are most appropriate to your situation.

- Environment and conditions for a successful retreat
  - Create an immersive experience outside of the typical schedule and setting. The goal is to withdraw from the distractions and routines of work and focus deeply on elements of the organization that normally exist beneath your conscious awareness.
  - Minimize distractions and competing priorities.
  - Address the authenticity issue explicitly. Stay away from making light of the retreat concept.
- Location and scheduling
  - The location conveys the dedicated purpose.
  - The atmosphere of the location is conducive to reduced distractions and increased focus.
  - Scheduling is structured but adaptable.
  - Location and scheduling are consistent with the values and resources available to your institution.
  - Logistics and scheduling are completed well ahead of time to minimize distractions.
  - Accessibility needs, facilities for skill development goals, dietary considerations, and so on are considered in advance.
  - Contingency plans are in place for emergencies, weather events, transportation issues, and so on.
- Program development
  - The program will be organized around a central theme or focus.
  - What are the advanced work expectations? Reading? Viewing? Anything else?
  - Use mixed approaches to maintain attention and productivity.
  - Aim for clear goals and outcomes!

- Consider group dynamics, including level of familiarity, trust, and collaboration. Do you need to include group-building work?
- Will you focus on knowledge, skills, culture, or dispositions? Will it be a combination of these?
- Focus on a competency-based mindset. What is the team already demonstrating? What comes next?
- Including activities, outdoor experiences, wellness activities, and so on can shape the overall environment of the work. Will these advance your goals?
- Including social time often enhances the interpersonal comfort level of the group.
- What technology requirements might you need?

- Facilitation and communication
  - Have the entire team arrive ready to participate in a focused and prepared manner.
  - Communicate clearly ahead of time within the team regarding the program, expectations, and outcomes.
  - Ensure constituents are aware of the purpose and program.
  - Examine how best to retain productive focus through effective facilitation (internal versus external facilitator).
  - Provide opportunities for feedback and debriefing on an ongoing basis.
- Outcomes for optimizing impact
  - Define a clear relationship between each activity and the anticipated outcomes of the retreat.
  - Articulate end-of-retreat expectations, including follow-up.
  - Discuss the observable implementation. What will this look like in practice?
  - Budget carefully and wisely. This is particularly important for public institutions who need to be mindful of public perceptions.
- Opportunities for follow-up
  - What are the expectations and opportunities for support once the team is back in their normal working environment?
  - Are there opportunities or expectations for ongoing reflection?
  - Provide opportunities for feedback and input regarding future events.
  - Evaluate observational details regarding outcomes. Did participants use the material developed at the retreat?

EPILOGUE

As discussed earlier in this book, brains retain and produce information in story form to draw context between related ideas (Storr, 2020). Therefore, you can employ an approach that makes use of this phenomenon. The introduction explained how the human brain uses story to organize, evaluate, and relate the most important elements of memory and consciousness. Throughout the book, you examined questions relating to your experience in becoming an educational leader. These questions certainly do not include the full measure of your important memories or associated values as an educational leader, but they do form the foundation for those memories. The idea is to challenge you to recall those stories that contain fundamental elements of what you believe and why you do what you do. Within these stories, and the many others that can stem from them, you will find the source of your volition. In other words, those stories that your brain has stored away are most valuable to you over your time as an educator.

An important element of ongoing and authentic reflection is to find the best way that works for you to recall those stories, to remind yourself of the main themes to be found within them, and to share them without hesitation. Add to these stories. Create your own list. Share stories with other colleagues, either within your leadership group or with others who do the same work in other districts. It is common to exchange stories with colleagues and friends, though generally within social contexts. These stories are powerful ways to explore our subconscious memories and beliefs, and a more structured and intentional approach is also a valuable way to remain aware of what motivates you to continue your work. The suggestion here, in the interest of practical implementation, is that you introduce more intentional and organized opportunities to reflect on these stories from your own experiences and share them with others in your work. A few practical suggestions might include periodic opportunities to share stories with other members of your school or district leadership team, to share your experiences with a new-teachers group in your district, or to include a writing prompt about an element of your experience as a leader on a specific topic (perhaps in a common area, such as the implementation of a districtwide initiative, or your experiences with a community challenge, such as reallocating scarce budget resources). By developing a common understanding of the role stories play in reflecting on values, you can create different opportunities to make use of them in the flow of your school year.

Those working in the field of educational leadership should also consider that maintaining your motivation usually dwells beneath your conscious awareness and is left to chance. Leaders recognize moments where they are either highly motivated or less motivated, but they rarely work on sustaining it. They simply ride the wave of motivation, basking in the highs and surviving the lows. Just like with health and capacity, they rarely find time to attend to it until the wheels come off, and they find themselves in a crisis. Disillusioned and unmotivated school leaders have a wide-ranging impact on the communities they lead, from disengagement and attrition to long-term detriments to implementing and maintaining substantive learning programs. Proactive maintenance and self-care are dismissed as a casualty of the challenging work leaders do. In writing this book, I argue that it need not be this way. The work is too challenging, and the price of turnover is too high.

So, just like with competitive athletes, you can turn your conscious attention to understanding what motivates you and nurture those parts of yourself as a foundational part of your effort to develop professionally. In my first book (Laliberte, 2025), I built a case for school leaders to address their physical, cognitive, emotional, and motivational capacity as a regular element of their professional learning. While I hope that book has helped many of my colleagues in leadership, I realized that the task of maintaining our motivation was a vastly different and more complex task than the other three elements. Your motivation lives within your subconscious mind, only occasionally peeking its head out in your more challenging moments. Thus, comes my desire to offer up this second book, to increase your awareness of, and your intentional support for, those ideas that drive you to the challenging work of leading schools. There is no shortage of information out there on attrition rates from school leadership positions, and anyone who has done the work knows that there are times when you wonder if you can continue (National Center for Education Statistics, 2023). Your work as a school leader is far too important to leave yourself vulnerable to avoidable elements like burnout and lack of motivation. By restoring the element of authenticity to your reflection and being aware of what motivates you, you can add quality and substance to your work experience to persevere through unexpected challenges.

If you are a school leader who is struggling to motivate yourself in the face of your challenges, I hope you have found the strategies within these pages helpful for reconnecting with your sense of purpose. There are no tricks or shortcuts to make the work easier. An intentional and deliberate approach is the best way to reprioritize your capacity and stay connected with your volition. Your task is to build tools and strategies to sustain yourself through difficult times, inspired by your broader sense of purpose and the rewards of all you do in the interest of student learning. You may not always see the outcomes of what you do, but please know that those outcomes are realized each day, and your students and staff are counting on you to continue your crucial work.

May you see your value and purpose within the challenges of each day.

REFERENCES AND RESOURCES

Albaladejo-Saura, M., Vaquero-Cristóbal, R., González-Gálvez, N., & Esparza-Ros, F. (2021). Relationship between biological maturation, physical fitness, and kinanthropometric variables of young athletes: A systematic review and meta-analysis. *International Journal of Environmental Research and Public Health, 18*(1), Article 328. https://doi.org/10.3390/ijerph18010328

Backman, I. (2023, October 9). *Stress amplifies the brain's ability to encode memory, new study finds.* Accessed at https://medicine.yale.edu/news-article/stress-amplifies-the-brains-ability-to-encode-memory-new-study-finds on November 12, 2025.

Balk, M. (2025, January 8). *50 personal values examples & how to live by yours* [Blog post]. Accessed at www.betterup.com/blog/personal-values-examples on November 13, 2025.

Bandhu, D., Mohan, M. M., Nittala, N. A. P., Jadhav, P., Bhadauria, A., & Saxena, K. K. (2024). Theories of motivation: A comprehensive analysis of human behavior drivers. *Acta Psychologica, 244,* Article 104177. https://doi.org/10.1016/j.actpsy.2024.104177

Bleidorn, W., & Hopwood, C. J. (2024). A motivational framework of personality development in late adulthood. *Current Opinion in Psychology, 55,* Article 101731. https://doi.org/10.1016/j.copsyc.2023.101731

Cherry, K. (2026, February 13). *Motivation: The driving force behind our actions.* Verywell Mind. Accessed at www.verywellmind.com/what-is-motivation-2795378 on November 12, 2025.

Clear, J. (n.d.). *Core values list.* Accessed at https://jamesclear.com/core-values on November 13, 2025.

Cleveland Clinic. (2022a, March 23). *Dopamine.* Accessed at https://my.clevelandclinic.org/health/articles/22581-dopamine on March 5, 2025.

Cleveland Clinic. (2022b, March 27). *Epinephrine (Adrenaline).* Accessed at https://my.clevelandclinic.org/health/articles/22611-epinephrine-adrenaline on October 10, 2025.

Cleveland Clinic. (2025, February 17). *Cortisol.* Accessed at https://my.clevelandclinic.org/health/articles/22187-cortisol on February 4, 2026.

Crum, A., & Crum, T. (2015, September 3). Stress can be a good thing if you know how to use it. *Harvard Business Review.* Accessed at https://hbr.org/2015/09/stress-can-be-a-good-thing-if-you-know-how-to-use-it on November 12, 2025.

DC Bar. (n.d.). *Values inventory.* Accessed at www.dcbar.org/getmedia/8aa1e92a-f5fa-4973-b104-709c6c55dbae/Clearing-Clutter-Handouts-1024191 on November 13, 2025.

Deci, E. L., Olafsen, A. H., & Ryan, R. M. (2017). Self-determination theory in work organizations: The state of a science. *Annual Review of Organizational Psychology and Organizational Behavior, 4,* 19–43. https://doi.org/10.1146/annurev-orgpsych-032516-113108

Dr. Ermshar & Associates. (2023). *The psychology of motivation: What drives human behavior?* [Blog post]. Accessed at www.drannetteermshar.com/the-psychology-of-motivation-what-drives-human-behavior on November 12, 2025.

Ebert, M. (2024, March 26). *A good principal knows when it's time to leave: How to end this chapter of your career gracefully.* Education Week. Accessed at www.edweek.org/leadership/opinion-a-good-principal-knows-when-its-time-to-leave/2024/03 on November 12, 2025.

Erikson, E. H. (1950). *Childhood and society.* Norton.

España, R. A., Schmeichel, B. E., & Berridge, C. W. (2016). Norepinephrine at the nexus of arousal, motivation and relapse. *Brain Research, 1641,* 207–216. https://doi.org/10.1016/j.brainres.2016.01.002

Falkowski, G. (2016, November). Boost mood and motivation naturally with 6 dopamine kick-starters. *MS Focus Magazine.* Accessed at https://msfocus.org/Magazine/Magazine-Items/Posted/Boost-mood,-motivation-with-dopamine-kick-starters on November 12, 2025.

Fishbach, A. (2018). How to keep working when you're just not feeling it. *Harvard Business Review.* Accessed at https://hbr.org/2018/11/how-to-keep-working-when-youre-just-not-feeling-it on November 13, 2025.

Frith, C. (2013). The psychology of volition. *Experimental Brain Research, 229,* 289–299. https://doi.org/10.1007/s00221-013-3407-6

Gavin, M. (2019, November 21). *Leadership self-assessment: How effective are you?* Harvard Business School. Accessed at https://online.hbs.edu/blog/post/leadership-self-assessment on November 12, 2025.

Generativity. (n.d.). In *Merriam-Webster's online dictionary.* Accessed at www.merriam-webster.com/dictionary/generativity on July 21, 2025.

Geneva Point Center. (2025, July 8). *Leadership training retreats: A complete guide to transforming your team*. Accessed at www.genevapoint.org/leadership-training-retreats-a-complete-guide-to-transforming-your-team on November 13, 2025.

Gleeson, B. (2023, June 21). Burden of command: How leaders identify and reduce burnout in themselves and their teams. *Forbes*. Accessed at www.forbes.com/sites/brentgleeson/2023/06/21/burden-of-command-how-leaders-identify-and-reduce-burnout-in-themselves-and-their-teams on November 12, 2025.

Gonzales. C. (2017). Decision-making: A cognitive science perspective. In S. E. F. Chipman (Ed.), *The Oxford handbook of cognitive science* (pp. 249–264). Oxford University Press.

Haggard, P. (2019). The neurocognitive bases of volition. *Annual Review of Psychology*, *70*, 9–28. https://doi.org/10.1146/annurev-psych-010418-103348

Halber, D. (2018, August 29). *Motivation: Why you do the things you do*. Accessed at www.brainfacts.org/thinking-sensing-and-behaving/learning-and-memory/2018/motivation-why-you-do-the-things-you-do-082818 on November 13, 2025.

Halloran, E. C. (2024). Adult development and associated health risks. *Journal of Patient-Centered Research and Reviews*, *11*(1), 63–67. https://doi.org/10.17294/2330-0698.2050

Hanel, P. H. P., Vione, K. C., Hahn, U., & Maio, G. R. (2017). Value instantiations: The missing link between values and behavior? In S. Roccas & L. Sagiv (Eds.), *Values and behavior: Taking a cross cultural perspective* (pp. 175–190). Springer.

Harvard University Center on the Developing Child. (2021, January 20). *InBrief: Understanding the science of motivation*. Accessed at https://developingchild.harvard.edu/resources/inbrief-understanding-the-science-of-motivation on November 13, 2025.

Hobart, P. J. (2020, January 29). *Where does motivation come from?* [Blog post]. Accessed at www.pamelajhobart.com/where-does-motivation-come-from on November 13, 2025.

Holmes, T. H., & Rahe, R. H. (1967). The social readjustment rating scale. *Journal of Psychosomatic Research*, *11*(2), 213–218.

Hook, B. (2025, July 27). *Two comprehensive lists of core values*. Accessed at https://values.institute/list-human-values on November 13, 2025.

Huberman, A. (2022, October 6). *Tools to manage dopamine and improve motivation and drive* [Blog post]. Accessed at www.hubermanlab.com/newsletter/tools-to-manage-dopamine-and-improve-motivation-and-drive on November 13, 2025.

Institute of Education Sciences. (2023, July 31). *Roughly one in ten public school principals left profession in 2021–22 school year*. Accessed at https://ies.ed.gov/learn/press-release/roughly-one-ten-public-school-principals-left-profession-2021-22-school-year on April 16, 2026.

Jeffrey, S. (2026, March 11). *The ultimate list of core values (over 230).* Accessed at https://scottjeffrey.com/core-values-list on March 31, 2026.

Jenkins, J. (2024, January 25). *Researchers establish brain pathway linking motivation, addiction and disease.* Accessed at https://news.njit.edu/researchers-establish-brain-pathway-linking-motivation-addiction-and-disease on November 13, 2025.

Jenson, C. (2024). *Triage your school: A physician's guide to preventing teacher burnout.* Solution Tree Press.

Jesse Owens Trust. (n.d.). *Jesse Owen's story.* Accessed at https://jesseowens.com/biography on November 13, 2025.

Julson, E. (2025, January 17). *10 best ways to increase dopamine levels naturally.* Healthline. Accessed at www.healthline.com/nutrition/how-to-increase-dopamine on November 13, 2025.

Kelly, J. (Writer) & Braff, Z. (Director). (2020, August 14). Biscuits (Season 1, Episode 2) [TV series episode]. In J. Sudeikis, B. Lawrence, B. Hunt, J. Kelly, J. Ingold, & B. Wrubel (Executive Producers), *Ted Lasso.* Ruby's Tuna; Universal Television; Doozer; Warner Brothers Television.

Kim, S. (2013). Neuroscientific model of motivational process. *Frontiers in Psychology, 4*, Article 98. https://doi.org/10.3389/fpsyg.2013.00098

Laliberte, S. A. (2025). *The school leader's game plan: Strategies for maximizing your capacity to tackle daily challenges.* Solution Tree Press.

Lee, J. (Writer) & Lipsey, M. (Director). (2023, April 12). Signs (Season 3, Episode 5) [TV series episode]. In J. Sudeikis, B. Lawrence, B. Hunt, J. Kelly, J. Ingold, B. Wrubel, J. Lee, J. Becker, & L. Katzer (Executive Producers), *Ted Lasso.* Ruby's Tuna; Universal Television; Doozer; Warner Brothers Television.

Lembke, A. (2021). *Dopamine nation: Finding balance in an age of indulgence.* Dutton Books.

Levin, S., & Bradley, K. (2019, March 19). *Understanding and addressing principal turnover: A review of the research.* National Association of Secondary School Principals, Learning Policy Institute. Accessed at https://learningpolicyinstitute.org/media/326/download?inline&file=NASSP_LPI_Principal_Turnover_Research_Review_REPORT.pdf on March 31, 2026.

Levontin, L., & Bardi, A. (2019). Using personal values to understand the motivational basis of amity goal orientation. *Frontiers in Psychology, 9*, Article 2736. https://doi.org/10.3389/fpsyg.2018.02736

Liljenström, H. (2022). Consciousness, decision making, and volition: Freedom beyond chance and necessity. *Theory in Biosciences, 141*, 125–140. https://doi.org/10.1007/s12064-021-00346-6

Machost, H., & Stains, M. (2023). Reflective practices in education: A primer for practitioners. *CBE Life Sciences Education, 22*(2), es2. https://doi.org/10.1187/cbe.22-07-0148

McIntyre, C. K., & Roozendaal, B. (2007). Adrenal stress hormones and enhanced memory for emotionally arousing experiences. In F. Bermúdez-Rattoni (Ed.), *Neural plasticity and memory: From genes to brain imaging.* Taylor & Francis. Accessed at www.ncbi.nlm.nih.gov/books/NBK3907 on November 13, 2025.

McLeod, S. (2025, October 15). *Erik Erikson's stages of psychosocial development* [Blog post]. Accessed at www.simplypsychology.org/erik-erikson.html on November 13, 2025.

McMahan, E. (2018). Developmental psychology: A microcosm of general psychology. *Eye on Psy Chi, 22*(4). https://doi.org/10.24839/2164-9812.Eye22.4.6

McMurray, C. (2021, March 4). *Why the brain loves stories* [Blog post]. Accessed at www.brainfacts.org/neuroscience-in-society/the-arts-and-the-brain/2021/why-the-brain-loves-stories-030421 on November 13, 2025.

Metivier, A. (2024, August 12). *Reflective thinking: 5 powerful strategies for improving your life.* Accessed at www.magneticmemorymethod.com/reflective-thinking on November 13, 2025.

Michigan Technical University. (n.d.). *Retreat planning.* Accessed at www.mtu.edu/student-leadership/student-orgs/rso-resources/transitions/retreatplanning.pdf on November 13, 2025.

Miller, A. (2023, May 31). How to harness your values to find motivation. *Forbes.* Accessed at www.forbes.com/councils/forbescoachescouncil/2023/05/31/how-to-harness-your-values-to-find-motivation on November 13, 2025.

Moss, J. (2019, December 11). Burnout is about your workplace, not your people. *Harvard Business Review.* Accessed at https://hbr.org/2019/12/burnout-is-about-your-workplace-not-your-people on November 13, 2025.

Motivation. (n.d.). In *Merriam-Webster's online dictionary.* Accessed at www.merriam-webster.com/dictionary/motivation on March 23, 2026.

National Center for Education Statistics. (2023, July 31). *Roughly one in ten public school principals left profession in 2021–22 school year* [Press release]. Accessed at https://ies.ed.gov/learn/press-release/roughly-one-ten-public-school-principals-left-profession-2021-22-school-year on November 13, 2025.

National Center for Education Statistics. (2024, May). *Principal turnover: Stayers, movers, and leavers.* Accessed at https://nces.ed.gov/programs/coe/indicator/slb on March 24, 2025.

NCSA College Recruiting. (2026, January 30). *NCAA transfer portal and rules.* Accessed at www.ncsasports.org/recruiting/ncaa-transfer-rules on February 21, 2026.

Neale, P. (2021, December 22). Seven tips for designing a leadership self-reflection practice. *Forbes.* Accessed at www.forbes.com/councils/forbescoachescouncil/2021/12/22/seven-tips-for-designing-a-leadership-self-reflection-practice on November 13, 2025.

Nonprofit Learning Lab. (2024, November 7). *Trauma informed facilitation: The power of reflection in training, workshops and experiences.* Accessed at www.nonprofitlearninglab.org/post-1/trauma-informed-facilitation-the-power-of-reflection-in-training-workshops-and-experiences on November 13, 2025.

O'Hara, D. (2017, December 18). *The intrinsic motivation of Richard Ryan and Edward Deci.* American Psychological Association. Accessed at www.apa.org/members/content/intrinsic-motivation on November 13, 2025.

Oléron, M. (2024, November 29). *Your exhaustive guide on corporate retreats* [Blog post]. Accessed at www.campfire-company.com/blog/your-exhaustive-guide-on-corporate-retreats on November 13, 2025.

Orenstein, G. A., & Kaur, J. (2022). *Erikson's stages of psychosocial development.* Accessed at www.ncbi.nlm.nih.gov/books/NBK556096 on November 13, 2025.

Patel, S. (2015). The science behind motivation. *Forbes.* Accessed at www.forbes.com/sites/sujanpatel/2015/01/09/the-science-behind-motivation on November 13, 2025.

Perry, E. (2023, August 8). *The meaning of personal values and how they impact your life* [Blog post]. Accessed at www.betterup.com/blog/meaning-of-personal-values on November 13, 2025.

Ponizovskiy, V., Grigoryan, L., Kühnen, U., & Boehnke, K. (2019). Social construction of the value-behavior relation. *Frontiers in Psychology, 10,* Article 934. https://doi.org/10.3389/fpsyg.2019.00934

Ray, J. (2025). *Finding your balance: Personal and professional wellness strategies for effective educational leadership.* Solution Tree Press.

Renken, E. (2020, April 11). *How stories connect and persuade us: Unleashing the brain power of narrative* [Blog post]. NPR. Accessed at www.npr.org/sections/health-shots/2020/04/11/815573198/how-stories-connect-and-persuade-us-unleashing-the-brain-power-of-narrative on November 13, 2025.

Saville, W. (2025, March 23) *Maturation.* Accessed at www.scienceforsport.com/maturation on February 14, 2026

Souders, B. (2019a, November 5). *20 most popular theories of motivation in psychology* [Blog post]. Accessed at https://positivepsychology.com/motivation-theories-psychology on January 19, 2025.

Souders, B. (2019b, November 5). *What motivates people? Exploring human behavior* [Blog post]. Accessed at https://positivepsychology.com/motivation-human-behavior on January 19, 2025.

Spiller, M. (2024, December 4). Dopamine rush—27 things to do instead of scroll [Blog post]. *Excursions Magazine.* Accessed at https://sanfordbehavioralhealth.com/2024/12/04/dopamine-rush-27-things-to-do-instead-of-scroll on July 17, 2025.

Stagnation. (n.d.). In *Merriam-Webster's online dictionary.* Accessed at www.merriam-webster.com/dictionary/stagnation on July 21, 2025.

Stanchfield, J. (2023, June 9). *Optimistic closing activities to celebrate, reflect, and connect to future learning* [Blog post]. Accessed at https://blog.experientialtools.com/2023/06/09/powerful-and-optimistic-closing-activities-to-celebrate-reflect-and-connect-to-future-learning on November 13, 2025.

Stones, M. (2020, May 7). How does age change sport performance? Master athletes have the answer. *Research Outreach.* Accessed at https://researchoutreach.org/articles/ageing-change-sport-performance-master-athletes-answer on February 14, 2026

Storr, W. (2020). *The science of storytelling: Why stories make us human and how to tell them better.* Abrams.

Suresh, T. (2024, July 15). *The complete guide to planning a successful company retreat* [Blog post]. Accessed at https://navan.com/blog/the-complete-guide-to-planning-a-successful-company-retreat on November 13, 2025.

Taha, L. (2021, January 29). *Jesse Owens: Olympic triumphs and Olympic-sized struggles.* Accessed at www.biography.com/athletes/jesse-owens-biography-olympic-triumphs-olympic-sized-struggles-20892201 on November 25, 2025.

Tyler, J., Boldi, M.-O., & Cherubini, M. (2022). Contemporary self-reflective practices: A large-scale survey. *Acta Psychologica, 230,* Article 103768. https://doi.org/10.1016/j.actpsy.2022.103768

UCLA Teaching and Learning Center. (2025, April). *Leveraging self-reflection to improve your teaching.* Accessed at https://teaching.ucla.edu/resources/teaching-guides/leveraging-self-reflection-to-improve-your-teaching on February 4, 2026.

USC Dornsife. (2023, November 17). *How liking your job will help you succeed.* Accessed at https://appliedpsychologydegree.usc.edu/blog/how-liking-your-job-will-help-you-succeed on July 8, 2025.

Volition. (n.d.). In *Merriam-Webster's online dictionary.* Accessed at www.merriam-webster.com/dictionary/volition on July 21, 2025.

Wang, F. (2025). Cognitive wellbeing of school principals: An uncharted territory. *Leadership and Policy in Schools,* 1–19. https://doi.org/10.1080/15700763.2025.2481500

Westover, J. H. (2024, January 11). *The power of storytelling: How our brains are wired for narratives.* Accessed at www.innovativehumancapital.com/article/the-power-of-storytelling-how-our-brains-are-wired-for-narratives on November 13, 2025.

Weststrate, N. M., & Glück, J. (2017). Hard-earned wisdom: Exploratory processing of difficult life experience is positively associated with wisdom. *Developmental Psychology, 53*(4), 800–814. https://doi.org/10.1037/dev0000286

INDEX

R

S

The School Leader's Game Plan
Scott A. Laliberte
Drawing parallels with competitive athletic training, Scott A. Laliberte provides school leaders with strategies and leadership resources for navigating daily challenges. He encourages leadership development through physical, mental, and emotional conditioning, empowering education leaders to sustain their well-being and effectiveness.
BKG235

Giving It Your All Without Giving It All
Blake Clark
This is the guide to the human side of leadership. Blake Clark offers a workbook approach to self-preservation and sustainability that will help every principal define their leadership identity and lead with authenticity. Gain practical strategies to conserve energy and make complex decisions with courage.
BKG304

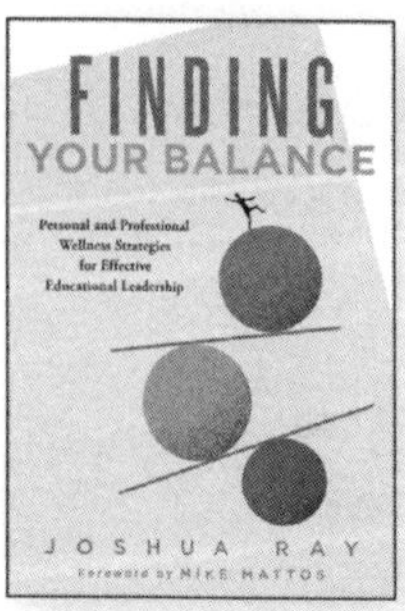

Finding Your Balance
Joshua Ray
Drawing on personal experiences, author Joshua Ray offers practical strategies, relatable anecdotes, and templates to help leaders thrive personally and professionally. Learn to prioritize work-life balance, overcome impostor syndrome, and lead intentionally, while discovering wellness strategies that help leaders be effective and efficient.
BKG250

The Principal's Backpack
Nancy Karlin Flynn
In The Principal's Backpack, Nancy Karlin Flynn draws on her background as a hiker and her years of experience leading schools to provide concrete ideas and practical tips on how to not only survive but thrive as a school leader.
BKG117